SCHOLASTIC

SEPTEMBER
Monthly Idea Book

Ready-to-Use Templates, Activities, Management Tools, and More—for Every Day of the Month

Karen Sevaly

New York • Toronto • London • Auckland • Sydney **Teaching**
Mexico City • New Delhi • Hong Kong • Buenos Aires *Resources*

DEDICATION

This book is dedicated to the teachers and staff of the Jurupa Unified School District. Their enthusiasm and earnest desire to motivate children has been a great inspiration. I am most grateful for the encouragement of my husband, Richard Sevaly, and our two sons, James and Robert.

Cover design by Maria Lilja
Cover art by Jillian Phillips
Interior design by Melinda Belter
Illustrations by Karen Sevaly

ISBN 978-0-545-37933-5

1 2 3 4 5 6 7 8 9 10   40   19 18 17 16 15 14 13

CONTENTS

FAVORITE TOPICS

ALL ABOUT ME

LET'S CELEBRATE BIRTHDAYS!

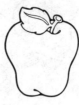

APPLE TIME

VIVA MEXICO!

NATIVE NORTH AMERICANS

AWARDS, INCENTIVES, AND MORE

ANSWER KEY

INTRODUCTION

Welcome to the original Monthly Idea Book series! This book was written especially for teachers getting ready to teach topics related to the month of September.

Each book in this month-by-month series is filled with dozens of ideas for PreK–3 classrooms. Activities connect to the Common Core State Standards for Reading (Foundational Skills), among other subjects, to help you meet the needs of your students. (For more information, see page 16.)

Most everything you need to prepare the lessons and activities in this resource is included, such as:

- calendar and weather-related props

- book cover patterns and stationery for writing assignments

- booklet patterns

- games and puzzles that support learning in curriculum areas such as math, science, and writing

- activity sheets that help students organize information, respond to learning, and explore topics in a meaningful way

- patterns for projects that connect to holidays, special occasions, and commemorative events

All year long, you can weave the ideas and reproducible patterns in these unique books into your monthly lesson plans and classroom activities. Happy teaching!

What's Inside

You'll find that this book is chock-full of reproducibles that make lesson planning easier:

- puppets and picture props

- bookmarks, booklets, and book covers

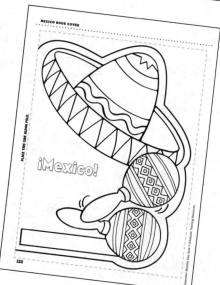

- game boards, puzzles, and word finds

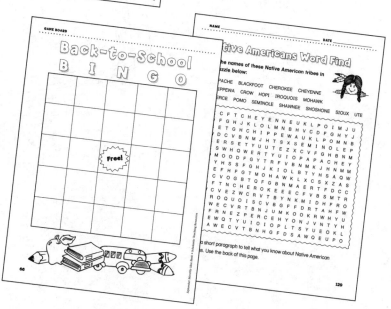

■ stationery

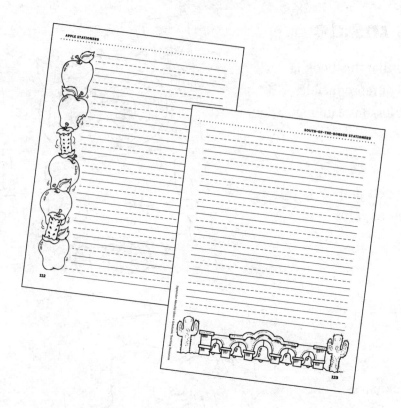

■ awards and certificates

How to Use This Book

The reproducible pages in this book have flexible use and may be modified to meet your particular classroom needs. Use the reproducible activity pages and patterns in conjunction with the suggested activities or weave them into your curriculum in other ways.

★ PHOTOCOPY OR SCAN

To get started, think about your developing lesson plans and upcoming bulletin boards. If desired, carefully remove the pages you will need. Duplicate those pages on copy paper, color paper, tagboard, or overhead transparency sheets. If you have access to a scanner, consider saving the pattern pages as PDF files. That way, you can size images up or down and customize them with text to create individualized lessons, center-time activities, interactive whiteboard lessons, homework pages, and more.

LAMINATE FOR DURABILITY

Laminating the reproducibles will help you extend their use. If you have access to a roll laminator, then you already know how fortunate you are when it comes to saving time and resources. If you don't have a laminator, clear adhesive vinyl covering works well. Just sandwich the pattern between two sheets of vinyl and cut off any excess. Then try some of these ideas:

- ■ Put laminated sheets of stationery in a writing center to use for handwriting practice. Wipe-off markers work great on coated pages and can easily be erased with dry tissue.

- ■ Add longevity to calendars, weather-related pictures, and pocket chart rebus pictures by preserving them with lamination.

- ■ Transform picture props into flannel board figures. After lamination, add a tab of hook-and-loop fastener to the back of the props and invite students to adhere them to the flannel board for storytelling fun.

- ■ To enliven magnet board activities, affix sections of magnet tape to the back of the picture props. Then encourage students to sort images according to the skills you're working on. For example, you might have them group images by commonalities such as initial sound, habitat, or physical attributes.

Coming Soon!

JANUARY - SNOWMAN CONTEST
FEBRUARY - SKATING PARTY
MARCH - KITE FLYING DAY
APRIL - EASTER VACATION
MAY - FLOWER SHOW
JUNE - SUMMER BEGINS

Wow!

★ BULLETIN BOARDS

1. Set the Stage

Use background paper colors that complement many themes and seasons. For example, the dark background you used as a spooky display in October will have dramatic effect in November, when you begin a unit on woodland animals or Thanksgiving.

While paper works well, there are other background options available. You might also try fabric from a colorful bed sheet or gingham material. Discontinued rolls of patterned wallpaper can be purchased at discount stores. What's more, newspapers are easy to use and readily available. Attach a background of comics to set off a lesson on riddles, or use grocery store flyers to provide food for thought on a bulletin board about nutrition.

2. Make the Display

The reproducible patterns in this book can be enlarged to fit your needs. When we say enlarge, we mean it! Think BIG! Use an overhead projector to enlarge the images you need to make your bulletin board extraordinary.

If your school has a stencil press, you're lucky. The rest of us can use these strategies for making headers and titles.

■ Cut strips of paper, cloud shapes, or cartoon bubbles. They will all look great! Then, by hand, write the text using wide-tipped permanent markers or tempera paint.

■ If you must cut individual letters, use 4- by 6-inch pieces of construction paper. (Laminate first, if you can.) Cut the uppercase letters as shown on page 14. No need to measure, as somewhat irregular letters will look creative, not messy.

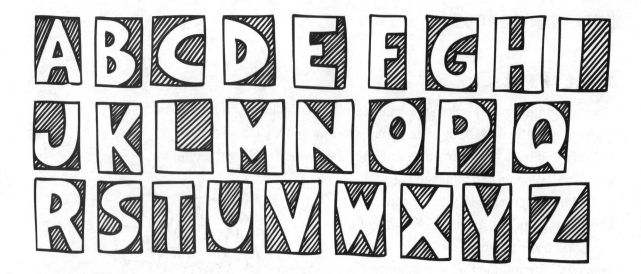

3. Add Color and Embellishments

Use your imagination! You'll be surprised at the great displays you can create.

- Watercolor markers work great on small areas. On larger areas, you can switch to crayons, color chalk, or pastels. (Lamination will keep the color off of you. No laminator? A little hairspray will do the trick as a fixative.)

- Cut character eyes and teeth from white paper and glue them in place. The features will really stand out and make your bulletin boards engaging.

- For special effects, include items that provide texture and visual interest, such as buttons, yarn, and lace. Try cellophane or blue glitter glue on water scenes. Consider using metallic wrapping paper or aluminum foil to add a bit of shimmer to stars and belt buckles.

- Finally, take a picture of your completed bulletin board. Store the photos in a recipe box or large sturdy envelope. Next year when you want to create the same display, you'll know right where everything goes. You might even want to supply students with pushpins and invite them to recreate the display, following your directions and using the photograph as support.

Staying Organized

Organizing materials with monthly file folders provides
you with a location to save reproducible activity pages and
patterns, along with related craft ideas, recipes, and magazine
or periodical articles.

If you prefer, use file boxes instead of folders. You'll find
that with boxes there will plenty of room to store enlarged
patterns, sample art projects, bulletin board materials, and
much more.

Meeting the Standards

CONNECTIONS TO THE COMMON CORE STATE STANDARDS

The Common Core State Standards Initiative (CCSSI) has outlined learning expectations in English/Language Arts, among other subject areas, for students at different grade levels. In general, the activities in this book align with the following standards for students in grades K–3. For more information, visit the CCSSI website at www.corestandards.org.

Reading: Foundational Skills

Print Concepts
- RF.K.1, RF.1.1. Demonstrate understanding of the organization and basic features of print.

Phonics and Word Recognition
- RF.K.3, RF.1.3, RF.2.3, RF.3.3. Know and apply grade-level phonics and word analysis skills in decoding words.

Fluency
- RF.K.4. Read emergent-reader texts with purpose and understanding.
- RF.1.4, RF.2.4, RF.3.4. Read with sufficient accuracy and fluency to support comprehension.

Writing

Production and Distribution of Writing
- W.3.4. Produce writing in which the development and organization are appropriate to task and purpose.
- W.K.5, W.1.5, W.2.5, W.3.5. Focus on a topic and strengthen writing as needed by revising and editing.

Research to Build and Present Knowledge
- W.K.7, W.1.7, W.2.7. Participate in shared research and writing projects.
- W.3.7. Conduct short research projects that build knowledge about a topic.
- W.K.8, W.1.8, W.2.8, W.3.8. Recall information from experiences or gather information from provided sources to answer a question.

Range of Writing
- W.3.10. Write routinely over extended time frames (time for research, reflection, and revision) and shorter time frames (a single sitting or a day or two) for a range of discipline-specific tasks, purposes, and audiences.

Speaking & Listening

Comprehension and Collaboration
- SL.K.1, SL.1.1, SL.2.1. Participate in collaborative conversations with diverse partners about grade-level topics and texts with peers and adults in small and larger groups.
- SL.K.2, SL.1.2, SL.2.2, SL.3.2. Recount or describe key ideas or details from a text read aloud or information presented orally or through other media.
- SL.K.3, SL.1.3, SL.2.3, SL.3.3. Ask and answer questions about what a speaker says in order to gather additional information or clarify something that is not understood.

Presentation of Knowledge and Ideas
- SL.K.4, SL.1.4, SL.2.4. Describe people, places, things, and events with relevant details, expressing ideas and feelings clearly.
- SL.K.5, SL.1.5, SL.2.5, SL.3.5. Add drawings or other visual displays to stories or recounts of experiences when appropriate to clarify ideas, thoughts, and feelings.

Language

Conventions of Standard English
- L.K.1, L.1.1, L.2.1, L.3.1. Demonstrate command of the conventions of standard English grammar and usage when writing or speaking.
- L.K.2, L.1.2, L.2.2, L.3.2. Demonstrate command of the conventions of standard English capitalization, punctuation, and spelling when writing.

Knowledge of Language
- L.2.3, L.3.3. Use knowledge of language and its conventions when writing, speaking, reading, or listening.

Vocabulary Acquisition and Use
- L.K.4, L.1.4, L.2.4, L.3.4. Determine or clarify the meaning of unknown and multiple-meaning words and phrases based on grade level reading and content, choosing flexibly from an array of strategies.
- L.K.6, L.1.6, L.2.6, L.3.6. Use words and phrases acquired through conversations, reading and being read to, and responding to texts.

CALENDAR TIME

Getting Started

September

Sunday	Monday	Tuesday	Wednesday	Thursday	Friday	Saturday

19

CALENDAR

MARK YOUR CALENDAR

Make photocopies of the calendar grid on page 19 and use it to meet your needs. Consider using the write-on spaces to:

- write the corresponding numerals for each day

- mark and count how many days have passed

- track the weather with stamps or stickers

- note student birthdays

- record homework assignments

- communicate with families about positive behaviors

- remind volunteers about schedules, field trips, shortened days, and so on

CELEBRATIONS THIS MONTH

Whether you post a photocopy of pages 20 though 23 near your class calendar or just turn to these pages for inspiration, you're sure to find lots of information on them to discuss with students. To take celebrating and learning a step further, invite the class to add more to the list. For example, students can add anniversaries of significant events and the birthdays of their favorite authors or historical figures.

CALENDAR HEADER

You can make a photocopy of the header on page 24, color it, and use it as a title for your classroom calendar. You might opt to give the coloring job to a student who has a birthday that month. The student is sure to enjoy seeing his or her artwork each and every day of the month.

BEFORE INTRODUCING WHAT'S THE WEATHER?

Make a photocopy of the body template on page 25. Laminate it so you can use it again and again. Before sharing the template with the class, cut out pieces of cloth in the shapes of clothing students typically wear this month. For example, if you live in a warm weather climate, your September attire might include shorts and t-shirts. If you live in chillier climates, your attire might include a scarf, hat, and coat. Fit the cutouts to the body outline. When the clothing props are made, and you're ready to have students dress the template, display the clothing. Invite the "weather helper of the day" to tell what pieces of clothing he or she would choose to dress appropriately for the weather. (For extra fun, use foam to cut out accessories such as an umbrella, sunhat, and raincoat.)

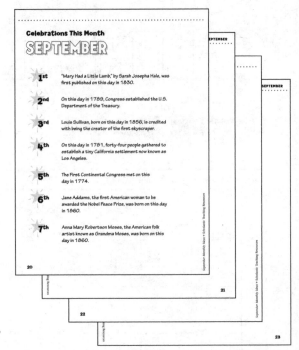

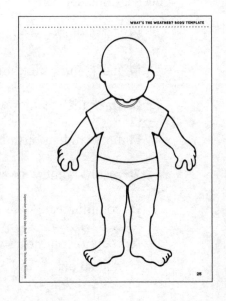

September

Sunday	Monday	Tuesday	Wednesday	Thursday	Friday	Saturday

Celebrations This Month

SEPTEMBER

 1st "Mary Had a Little Lamb," by Sarah Josepha Hale, was first published on this day in 1830.

 2nd On this day in 1789, Congress established the U.S. Department of the Treasury.

 3rd Louis Sullivan, born on this day in 1856, is credited with being the creator of the first skyscraper.

 4th On this day in 1781, forty-four people gathered to establish a tiny California settlement now known as Los Angeles.

 5th The First Continental Congress met on this day in 1774.

 6th Jane Addams, the first American woman to be awarded the Nobel Peace Prize, was born on this day in 1860.

 7th Anna Mary Robertson Moses, the American folk artist known as Grandma Moses, was born on this day in 1860.

8th   Today is International Literacy Day, a time to highlight the importance of literacy to individuals around the world.

9th   On this day in 1836, Abraham Lincoln was issued a license to practice law in Illinois.

10th   Born in Puerto Rico on this day in 1945, Jose Feliciano overcame his blindness to become one the most accomplished guitarists in the world.

11th   The English explorer Henry Hudson discovered Manhattan Island on this date in 1609.

12th   Jesse Owens, acclaimed American Olympic athlete, was born on this day in 1913.

13th   On this day in 1948, Margaret Chase Smith was elected to the U. S. Senate, becoming the first woman to serve in both houses of Congress.

14th   Francis Scott Key wrote the words to "The Star Spangled Banner" on this day in 1814.

15th   National Hispanic Heritage Month begins on this day and is celebrated until October 15.

16th Independence Day in Mexico is observed on this day to celebrate its freedom from Spain. Viva Mexico!

17th Today is Citizenship Day in honor of the anniversary of the signing of the U.S. Constitution.

18th George Washington laid the cornerstone of the U.S. Capitol in Washington, D.C. on this day in 1793.

19th Ahoy, matey! International Talk Like a Pirate Day is observed on this day in many countries.

20th On this day in 1519, the famous explorer Ferdinand Magellan set sail from Spain in search of a western sea route to the Spice Islands.

21st In the Southern Hemisphere, the people of Argentina celebrate the beginning of Spring on this day!

22nd Italo Marchiony filed an application to patent the ice-cream cone on this day in 1903.

23rd On this day in 1846, a German astronomer discovered Neptune, the eighth planet from the sun.

24th The Muppets creator Jim Henson was born on this day in 1936.

25th Extra! Extra! Read all about it! On this day in 1690, America's first newspaper was published in Boston, Massachusetts.

26th John Chapman, better known as Johnny Appleseed, was born on this day in 1774.

27th It's Ancestor Appreciation Day, a time to celebrate your family's history.

28th Today marks the birthday of the great Chinese teacher, Confucius, who was born in 551 BC.

29th On this day in 1988, Stacy Allison became the first American woman to climb Mount Everest, the highest place on earth.

30th In 1927, Babe Ruth made baseball history on this day by hitting his 60th home run of the season.

Other important occurrences this month include:

LABOR DAY (celebrated the first Monday in September)

GRANDPARENT'S DAY (observed the first Sunday of September following Labor Day)

ROSH HASHANAH (the Jewish New Year, celebrated on the first two days of Tishri, the seventh month of the Jewish calendar)

NATIONAL HISPANIC HERITAGE MONTH (observed from September 15th to October 15th)

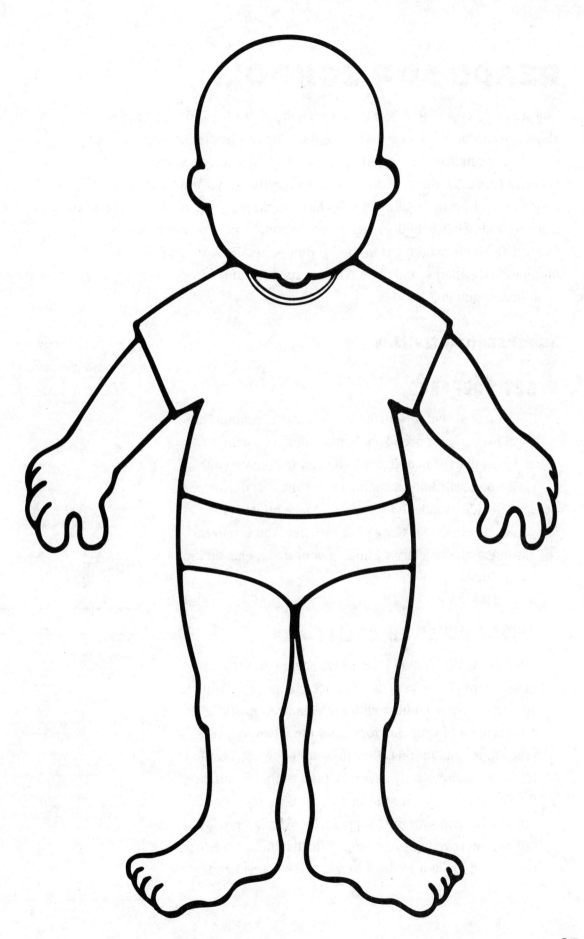

READY FOR SCHOOL!

The start of a new school year brings excitement, anticipation, and many challenges for both teachers and students, whether they're newcomers or returning to familiar territory and routines. Organization and preparation is key in launching the year in a positive, proactive way. From setting up your classroom and establishing rules to preparing for substitute or student teachers and helping children feel welcome and "at home," you'll find a treasure trove of useful items in this section—checklists, student passes, mini-posters, patterns, and more. Time to rev up and get ready for a great new beginning!

Suggested Activities

GET PREPARED

Copy page 37 and review the items in each section. This checklist can be a useful guide in helping you gather and organize the materials you'll need to prepare your classroom, schedule, and students for the first day of school and beyond. To use, simply check off each item as you complete the task or gather supplies. You can even customize the checklist by adding your own items on the blank lines.

"FIRST DAYS" CHECKLIST

The handy checklist on page 38 will help you keep track of the many "introductions" you need to make to help students become familiar with the organization and arrangement of your classroom and the schedules, rules, procedures, and routines they need to follow. You can fill in any additional items on the lines at the bottom of the list. As you plan for the first week of school, consider introducing items on the list gradually over several days rather than covering everything with students on the first day, which might lead them to feel overwhelmed and

stressed. Keep in mind that you have the entire school year, so take time during these first days to enjoy introducing students to their new classroom "home" and helping them feel at ease with all the exciting things that await them.

★ DOOR HANGERS

Welcome students to your room with the adorable door hanger on page 39. To prepare, copy the sign onto tagboard, or glue it to sturdy cardboard and trim to fit. Color it with bright markers and laminate for durability. Then cut out the circle where indicated and slide it over the doorknob. You might also prepare the "Please Do Not Disturb!" door hanger on page 40 to display when students are hard at work. If desired, you can glue the two hangers back-to-back, with sturdy cardboard sandwiched between them, to create a double-sided hanger.

★ FROM SCHOOL TO HOME

Copy and cut out the transportation tags (page 41) and have them ready to fill out on the first day of school, or fill them out in advance if you know each child's mode of transportation. If desired, laminate the tags, punch a hole in the top of each, and add a length of yarn to create necklaces for kids to wear. Use the tags to help group children for departure at the end of the day. Be sure to collect the tags as children board their rides or leave the school grounds.

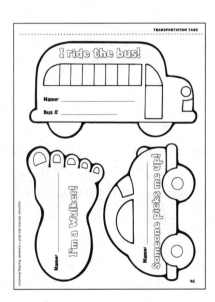

READY-TO-GO PASSES

Prepare a supply of the student passes on page 42 to keep on hand for a quick way to give kids permission to leave the room. Program the passes, then laminate them for durability. If desired, you can use a wipe-off pen to fill in the open-ended pass. To help children keep hold of their passes, use yarn to create necklaces that they can wear around their necks. Or glue a clothespin to the back of each pass and clip it onto the child's shirt.

 COMMUNICATION TAGS

The tags on page 43 make useful tools for helping children express the need for help or to share their accomplishments and ideas. Copy a supply of the tags, laminate, and place them in a basket along with wipe-off pens. Put the basket in an area that's easily accessible to students, or prepare an individual set of tags for children to keep in their personal workspace. Encourage students to fill out the tags, as needed, then hold them up or display them in a specific area.

 CLASSROOM CODE OF CONDUCT

One way to successfully manage your classroom is to establish a code of conduct. During the first days of school, discuss the elements of good class behavior with students. Write their responses and ideas on the chalkboard. Then work with students to come up with a classroom code of conduct. Keep the final list to ten or fewer items, and help children phrase each one in positive terms (avoid using *don't*). Copy the list onto poster board, leaving space around the edges for students to sign their names. If desired, make an enlarged copy of the mini-poster (page 44) to glue to poster board. Display the poster in a conspicuous place to help remind students of their agreement to work together to create a peaceful, pleasant, and productive environment in which all can learn and grow.

★ BACK-TO-SCHOOL PICTURE PROPS

Copy, color, and cut out the patterns on pages 45–50. There are numerous uses for these, such as name tags, calendar symbols, patterning practice, or matching activities. You might also use an overhead projector to trace large images of the patterns onto poster board or bulletin board paper. Color, cut out, and use the images to create displays or signs to post around the room.

★ CALENDAR BULLETIN BOARD

Create a year-round calendar display that you can change and customize for each month of the school year. First, select a bulletin board or display area spacious enough to accommodate a large 5- by 7-square calendar grid. You might use 8-inch squares of construction paper to create the grid. Number the squares from 1 to 31, and cut several extra squares to leave blank. Laminate the squares, then arrange them on the display to represent the current month. Add the days of the week and the name of the month, attach calendar symbols or fill in special days and events, and the calendar is ready for use!

CLASSROOM CRITTERS

Enlarge the cute critters on pages 51–54 to use in any number of ways, such as to label learning centers, group students, display work, adorn bulletin boards, and create signs. To make a friendly welcome sign for your classroom, simply copy the image of one of the characters onto poster board, add "Welcome!" along with your name and room number, then attach the sign to your door. As they are, the patterns make great booklet covers and creative writing pages. However you choose to use them, you'll find these critters help liven up any classroom environment!

POCKETS FULL OF HELPERS

Prepare these easy-to-use overalls as a helpers' chart. To begin, transfer the image of the overalls (page 55) onto light blue poster board. Write the name of a classroom job on each pocket. Laminate and cut slits along the top line of each pocket, then display in a prominent place in the room. You might label squares of fabric with student names to serve as handkerchiefs that can be tucked into the slits when assigning jobs.

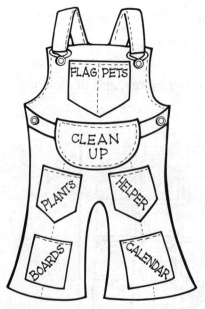

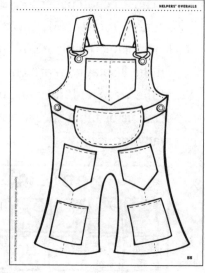

★ OWL PUPPET

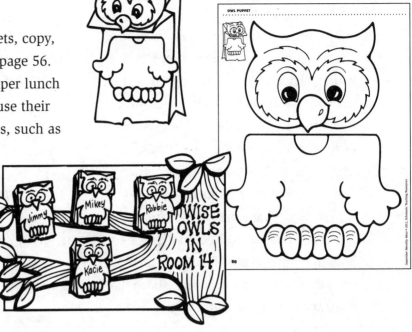

To make these adorable owl puppets, copy, color, and cut out the patterns on page 56. Glue the two pieces to a brown paper lunch bag, as shown. Invite children to use their puppets to act out school scenarios, such as making new friends, doing class activities, or playing a game at recess. To use the owls on a bulletin board display, create a paper tree with branches, attach the owls to the branches, and add a title.

★ ALPHABET OWL

Kids can keep this special owl on hand as a guide to recognizing and writing the letters of the alphabet. To prepare, copy a supply of the owl pattern on page 57. Invite children to cut out their owl, write their name on it, and color as desired. Then collect the owls and laminate them. You might attach the owls to children's desks or allow kids to keep their owl with their personal belongings so they can have access to the alphabet chart at school or home.

★ NUMBER BEAR

Invite children to make a stand-up "number bear" to use as reference for counting and writing their numbers. Copy a class supply of the bear pattern (page 58) onto tagboard. Have children color and cut out their bear and label it with their name. Then help them cut along the lines on each side of the legs, as shown, and fold along the dashed line to create a stand. Children can stand the bear on their desks and use it as a guide in counting and number activities.

"BEARY" GOOD!

Use these movable bears to show off children's work around the room. To make, have children color and cut out the patterns (pages 59–60). Then show them how to assemble the bear with brass fasteners, attaching the head, arms, and legs to the body where indicated. Have children write their name on their bear. When displaying work, invite children to pose their bear as desired, using tape to hold the limbs in position. They might have their bear hold the work above its head, in front of its chest, or even position their bear dancing atop it.

BRAGGING ROBOTS

Convert plain 9- by 12-inch sheets of construction paper into boastful robots with the patterns on page 61. First, copy the patterns onto colorful paper. (You might use a different color for the head, arms, and feet.) Cut out the patterns and glue each one to construction paper to create a robot, as shown. Laminate and display several  robots along with a sentence strip labeled with the title of this activity. Whenever you want to recognize a child's work, simply attach it to a robot on the display.

HOMEWORK AWARDS

As you kick off a new year, try this idea to encourage students to turn in their homework. Each day, collect all homework assignments in a large colorful basket. Once all the assignments are in, close your eyes and randomly select one student's paper from the basket. Call out the lucky child's name and award that student a small prize, or award a special privilege for the day. You'll find that children will eagerly turn in completed homework assignments for a chance to earn a special treat!

★ HOMEWORK NIBBLES

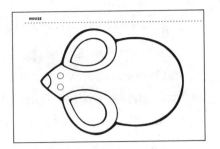

This motivational display will also encourage students to complete and turn in homework assignments. After marking and labeling the days of the week across the top of the display, cut out a mouse pattern (page 62) and a wedge of paper cheese for each child. (For cheese, cut out triangular shapes from yellow paper and punch holes in each one.) Then stretch a length of yarn across the display for each child, attaching each end with a pushpin. Add a mouse to the left side of each yarn line and a cheese wedge to the right side. As children turn in homework during the week, have them move their mice across the board. Using this display helps children easily keep track of homework assignments that need to be or have been turned in. If desired, reward children who have completed all homework for the week with a special treat on Friday.

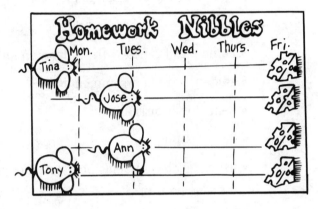

★ STUDENT BEHAVIOR REPORTS

The reproducible report (page 62) provides a quick and easy way to communicate with families about children's behavior and work habits. To use, copy and complete a chart for each child. You might discuss the chart with children and use feedback they offer about their own behavior when filling out the report. Send the reports home with the request that parents or guardians sign and return them the next school day. File the returned reports to document student progress and have on hand for parent/guardian conferences, as well as to review progress (or setbacks) with students. As needed, set up times to discuss children's behavioral issues or progress by phone or in person with parents or guardians.

TIME FOR A SUBSTITUTE

There's no time like the present to prepare for the inevitable—the day you'll need a substitute teacher. To be ready for this event (or to prepare for a student teacher assigned to your class), provide a file box or special folder filled with useful information and items such as the following:

- a class list, noting students with special needs

- class rules and discipline procedures

- daily class schedule and duty schedule

- name tags labeled with students' names

- student seating assignments

- behavior awards and stickers

- daily lesson plan

- list of reliable students and staff members who can be called on, if needed

- good behavior awards or treats to be given to students at the end of the day

- variety of worksheets appropriate for the skill level and abilities of your students (include a class supply of each one)

- a list of games, complete with instructions, that can be easily explained and played with students (also note where the games are located)

- a list of creative writing topics and a class supply of stationery to use for writing assignments (see page 63)

- note paper or special forms that can be used to devise a daily report during your absence

- several storybooks that can be read to the class

- a clean coffee mug, tea bags, non-perishable treats, and so on, for the substitute's use

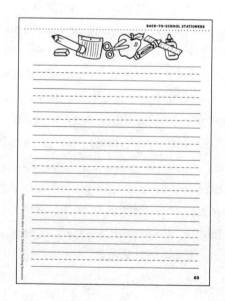

GETTING TO KNOW YOU

Provide a name tag (page 64) for your substitute or student teacher to wear while in class. As an introduction, and to help establish a friendly relationship with students, you might suggest that the teacher use a simple guessing game about his or her favorite color, hobbies, favorite school subjects, pets, favorite food, and so on. After listing the students' guesses, the teacher can then reveal the actual facts about himself or herself. Students will be delighted—or dismayed—to learn how many things they guessed right.

TWO-PART STUDENT AWARD

Copy a class supply of the award on page 64 for your substitute or student teacher to use to recognize students for helping make the day go well. To use, the teacher simply fills out both sides of the award for a child. Then he or she cuts the two sections apart, gives the left section to the child to take home, and leaves the right section for your information.

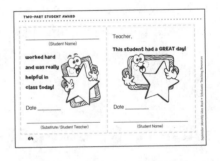

STUDENT DETECTIVES

The reproducible on page 65 is a fun activity to do anytime, but is ideal for having on hand for use by a substitute or student teacher. Simply copy a class supply of the page and distribute to students to complete. The questions give students an opportunity to explore information, make observations, and share what they know about classmates, the classroom, schedules, and procedures. When finished, children can share and compare their responses.

★ BACK-TO-SCHOOL BINGO

Have fun playing Bingo as a whole class. First, work with the class to brainstorm a list of words related to school. Then make several copies of the Bingo game board (page 66) and fill in words from the list, using different words on each game board. Also, write each word on a plain index card. Copy the programmed game boards, enough for each student in a group (or the whole class) to have one, then laminate the boards and word cards. To use, supply players with Bingo chips or dried beans to use as markers, then have a caller choose one word card at a time to read to players. If players have that word on their game board, they cover it with a marker. Continue play until players have covered all of the words on their game boards. At that time, all the players call out "Bingo!" together.

★ BACK-TO-SCHOOL WORD FIND

Reinforce students' developing vocabulary with the school-related word find on page 67. Explain that each word in the puzzle reads across from left to right, or down from top to bottom (there are no diagonal or backward words). Then have children try to find all of the words in the word bank, circling each as they find it. After students have found all the words, you might have them use six of the words to write a paragraph as indicated at the bottom of the sheet. When finished, you may want to add the words to your class word wall, then encourage students to use them in their creative writing assignments.

GET PREPARED CHECKLIST

**Use this checklist to get ready for the first day of school.
Add your own items, as desired.**

ROOM ENVIRONMENT

- ❏ Decorate bulletin boards
- ❏ Prepare and post:
  - ❏ Welcome sign
  - ❏ Your name and room number
  - ❏ Class schedule
  - ❏ Class rules
  - ❏ _____
  - ❏ _____
  - ❏ _____
- ❏ Arrange classroom
  - ❏ Student desks/tables
  - ❏ Learning centers
  - ❏ Display areas
  - ❏ _____
  - ❏ _____

SUPPLIES

- ❏ Purchase or obtain the following:
  - ❏ Writing paper
  - ❏ Drawing paper
  - ❏ Construction paper
  - ❏ Pencils and pens
  - ❏ Crayons
  - ❏ Colored markers
  - ❏ Glue and glue sticks
  - ❏ Paper clips
  - ❏ Stapler and staples
  - ❏ Tape
  - ❏ Pushpins
- ❏ File folders
- ❏ Rulers
- ❏ Art supplies
- ❏ Lesson plan book
- ❏ Grade book
- ❏ Attendance materials
- ❏ _____
- ❏ _____
- ❏ _____
- ❏ _____

STUDENT PREPARATIONS

- ❏ Make student name tags
- ❏ Prepare student transportation tags
- ❏ Prepare take-home packets:
  - ❏ Student Information Form
  - ❏ Emergency Card
  - ❏ Bus regulations
  - ❏ Letter to parents
  - ❏ Class supply list
  - ❏ Class schedule
  - ❏ _____
  - ❏ _____
- ❏ Check student records for special needs, medical conditions, and so on
- ❏ Prepare individualized "Welcome to School" cards
- ❏ _____
- ❏ _____

GETTING ORGANIZED

- ❏ Prepare a class list
- ❏ Create a seating chart
- ❏ Become familiar with emergency procedures
- ❏ For the first week:
  - ❏ Write lesson plans
  - ❏ Prepare needed materials for lessons
  - ❏ _____
  - ❏ _____
- ❏ Create files for:
  - ❏ Parent correspondence
  - ❏ School bulletins
  - ❏ Substitute teacher
  - ❏ _____
  - ❏ _____
- ❏ _____
- ❏ _____
- ❏ _____
- ❏ _____

"FIRST DAYS" CHECKLIST

❑ Review the class and school rules as well as the discipline policy.

❑ Review learning centers, the care and storage of classroom supplies, and of any equipment students will use.

❑ Explain the homework policies and expectations.

❑ Explain your classroom helpers system.

❑ Distribute textbooks and materials, and discuss their use and care.

❑ Issue pencils, crayons, rulers, and other appropriate student materials.

❑ Explain the procedures for collecting and passing out materials, supplies, and assignments.

❑ Check on students' lunch arrangements (do this *before* lunch time).

❑ Explain the cafeteria procedures and rules.

❑ Check on students' transportation arrangements and review dismissal procedures.

❑ Review the procedures and rules for the gym, playground, and recess.

❑ Tour the school campus and grounds and introduce students to school personnel.

❑ Conduct "Getting to Know You" activities to help students learn about each other.

❑ Discuss students' expectations for the new school year.

❑ Review the procedures for class rewards, celebration events, and field trips.

❑ Pass out materials that students need to take home. Point out forms that should be signed by parents/guardians and returned the next school day.

❑ _____

❑ _____

❑ _____

CUT OUT.

Hello!

Welcome to

_____

classroom

ROOM _____

CUT OUT.

Shhhh

Please
Do Not
Disturb.

We're WORKING!

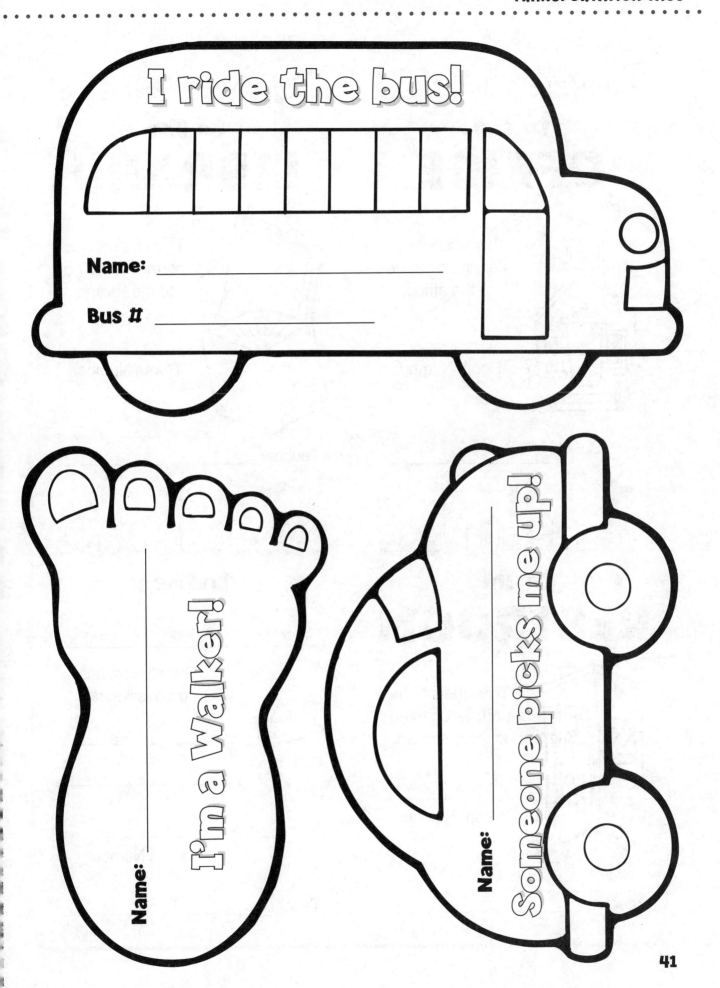

I ride the bus!

Name: _____

Bus # _____

I'm a Walker!

Name: _____

Someone picks me up!

Name: _____

Student Pass
to the
OFFICE

This student has
permission to go
to the office.

_____
Room Number

Teacher _____

Student Pass
to the
LIBRARY

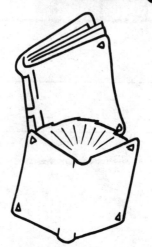

This student has
permission to go
to the library.

_____
Room Number

Teacher _____

Student Pass
to the
RESTROOM

This student has
permission to go
to the restroom.

_____
Room Number

Teacher _____

Student Pass
to the

_____

This student has
permission to

_____

_____

_____
Room Number

Teacher _____

I have a problem!

The problem is:

_____

_____

_____

_____

_____
Name

_____
Date

I need HELP!

I need help with:

_____

_____

_____

_____

_____
Name

_____
Date

I have something GOOD to report!

It is: _____

_____

_____

_____

_____
Name

_____
Date

I have a suggestion!

_____

_____

_____

_____

_____

_____
Name

_____
Date

_____'s Classroom

Code of Conduct

1. Be polite at all times.

2. Work quietly to avoid disturbing others.

3. Listen courteously when others are speaking.

4. Be friendly and helpful to classmates.

5. Be truthful and honest.

6. Respect teachers and other adults.

7. Be prepared for class every day.

8. Arrive to class on time.

9. Cooperate with others.

10. Always do your best.

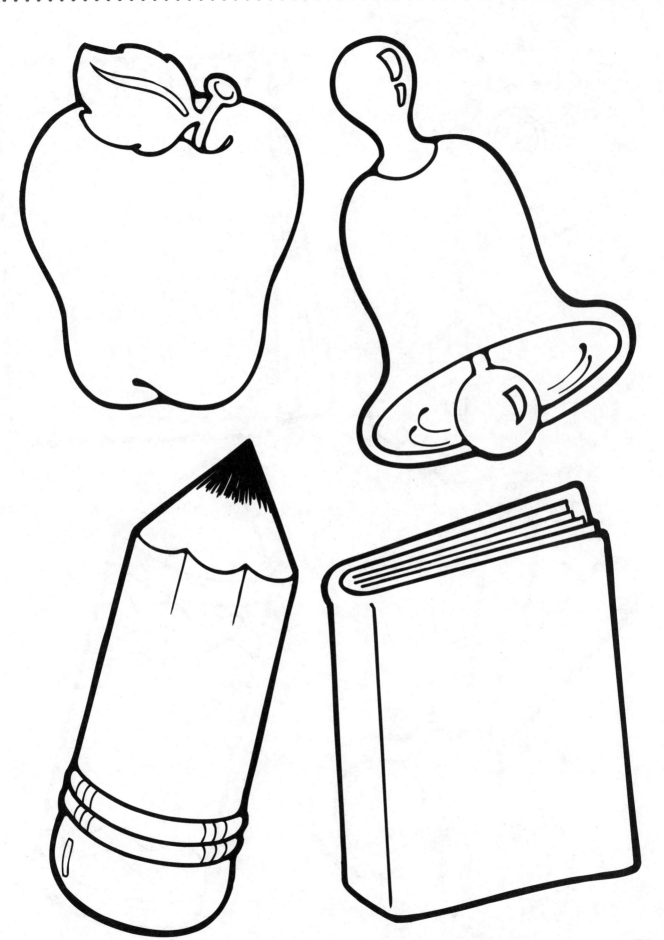

September Monthly Idea Book © Scholastic Teaching Resources

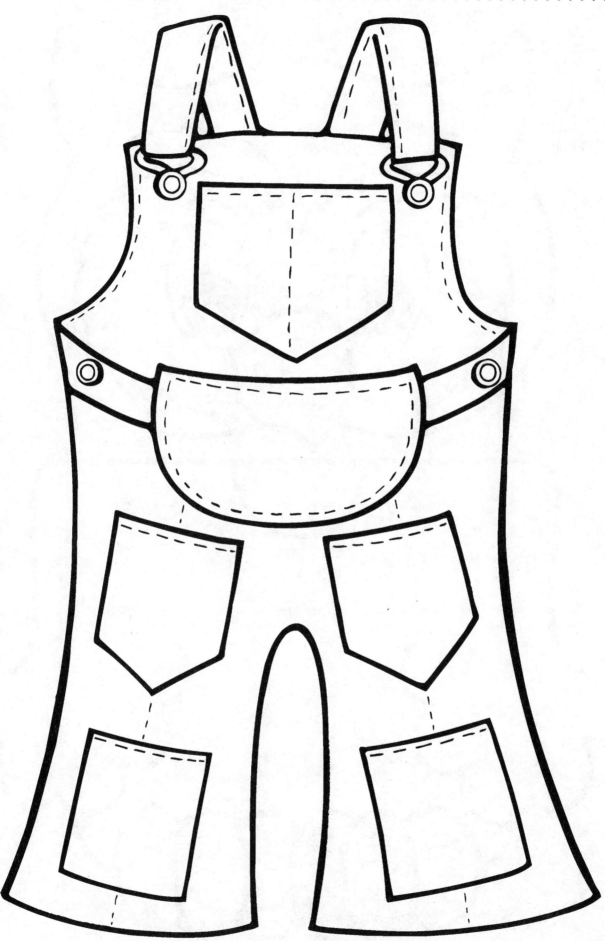

September Monthly Idea Book © Scholastic Teaching Resources

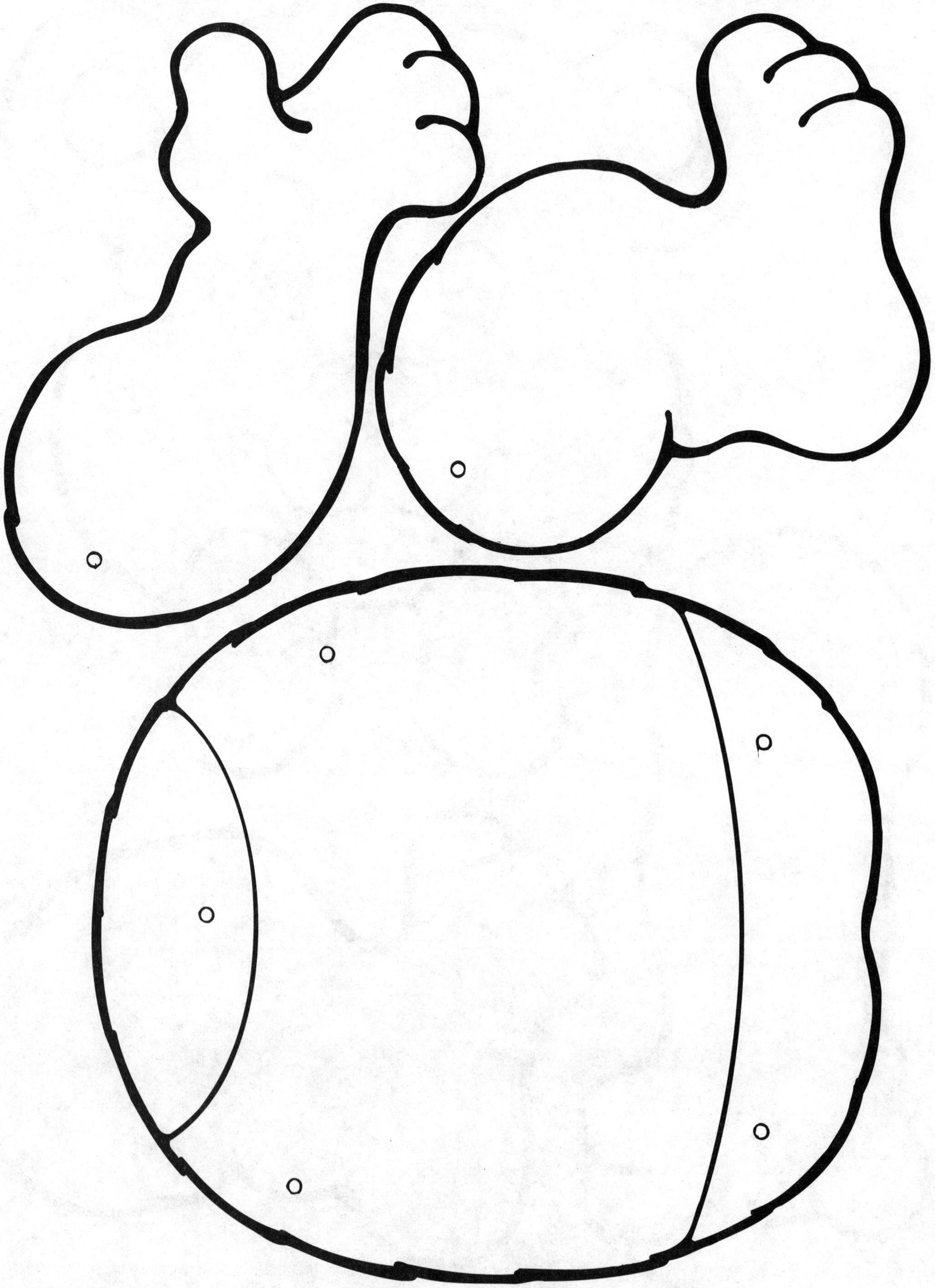

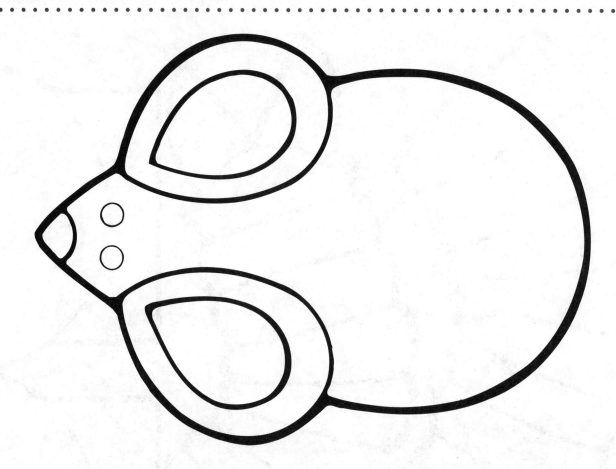

Student Behavior Report

Name _____ Date _____

	Excellent	Good	Improving	Needs Work
Overall Behavior	❑	❑	❑	❑
Follows Directions	❑	❑	❑	❑
Completes Work	❑	❑	❑	❑
Follows Rules	❑	❑	❑	❑
Cooperates	❑	❑	❑	❑
Shows Self-Control	❑	❑	❑	❑

Parent/Guardian: Please sign and return this report on the next school day. Write any comments on the back.

Teacher _____ Parent/Guardian Signature _____

My Name is . . .

_____

_____

TWO-PART STUDENT AWARD

_____
(Student Name)

worked hard and was really helpful in class today!

Date _____

_____
(Substitute/Student Teacher)

Teacher,

This student had a GREAT day!

Date _____

_____
(Student Name)

Student Detective

Discover fun things about your class and classmates.
Write your answers on the lines.

1. How many?   desks _____   tables _____   chairs _____

2. How many?   doors _____   windows _____   bulletin boards _____

3. How many?   girls _____   boys _____   students in all _____

4. How many students have the following?

   brown eyes _____   green eyes _____   blue eyes _____

   blonde hair _____   red hair _____   brown or black hair _____

5. Find your name around the room. How many times did you see it? _____

6. Do any students share the same first or last name? Write their names:

   _____

   _____

7. What time does each activity start?

   school _____   lunch _____   recess _____

8. Do you know the name of each? Write it.

   your school _____

   your teacher _____

   the principal _____

9. What is your favorite class rule? Write it here.

   _____

   _____

10. Pick one. How many books about that topic can you find in the room?

   dinosaurs _____   mice _____   bears _____

Back-to-School
B I N G O

Free!

Back-to-School Word Find

Find these words in the puzzle below:

ART CLASS EDUCATION HOMEWORK MATH MUSIC
PLAYGROUND PRINCIPAL READING SCHOOL SCIENCE
SPELLING STUDENTS STUDY TEACHER WRITING

```
A  S  D  F  R  T  H  K  L  P  I  O  S  C  H  O  O  L  D  T
W  E  F  G  T  Y  H  J  E  D  U  C  A  T  I  O  N  W  E  H
Q  W  E  F  E  L  F  D  F  G  T  Y  H  U  J  I  K  O  U  O
P  R  T  B  A  S  C  L  A  S  S  T  H  N  M  V  X  Z  S  M
R  T  E  R  C  V  T  Y  U  S  P  E  L  L  I  N  G  L  I  E
I  W  Q  D  H  R  P  L  A  Y  G  R  O  U  N  D  Y  B  R  W
N  S  C  I  E  N  C  E  G  H  J  K  V  M  C  D  R  T  Y  O
C  Y  H  F  R  T  N  L  P  S  T  U  D  E  N  T  S  F  G  R
I  Y  H  J  T  M  H  U  K  A  R  T  T  H  J  U  T  F  R  K
P  D  R  G  H  A  D  F  D  R  T  Y  U  J  N  M  U  H  U  L
A  W  R  I  T  I  N  G  J  U  M  A  T  H  G  Y  D  H  U  J
L  T  H  U  J  K  I  S  C  F  T  V  G  S  E  R  Y  G  M  R
R  E  A  D  I  N  G  G  H  N  V  X  Z  A  M  U  S  I  C  W
K  D  M  S  D  V  B  G  T  R  E  W  Q  X  C  V  B  N  M  J
```

Using six words from the puzzle, write a short paragraph about a
day at school. If you need more space, use the back of this page.

_____

_____

_____

_____

September Monthly Idea Book © Scholastic Teaching Resources

ALL ABOUT ME

There's one topic most students excel in—sharing about themselves! Take the opportunity to capitalize on students' "self-interest" with activities that help them explore their names, unique characteristics and traits, relationships with others, families, and personal information. Activities also help build feelings of community as students learn about and connect with others in the class.

Suggested Activities

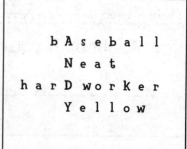

★ NAME HEADBANDS

Students read, write, and hear their names many times a day. Invite students to wear simple headbands as they learn about their own and others' names. Measure a 2-inch-wide strip of laminated tagboard or construction paper trimmed to fit each child's head, staple the ends together, and write the child's name on the front. Have students use their headbands for these activities:

- Find classmates whose names begin with the same letter.

- Choose a letter, then find classmates whose names have that letter.

- Look for others who share the same first (or last) name.

- Read the headbands to discover if there are any names that rhyme.

- Find the person with the shortest or longest name.

- Search names to find smaller words "hidden" in them.

- Work in small groups to alphabetize their names.

★ "ABOUT ME" ACROSTICS

Invite students to create acrostics with their names. First, have them write the letters of their first name down the center of a sheet of paper. Then have them use each letter in a word or phrase that describes or tells something about them, such as a personal trait, or a favorite color, food, movie, hobby, and so on. More advanced students might make acrostics of their first and last names. When finished, have students share their acrostics with classmates, then display them on a bulletin board with the title of this activity.

```
b A s e b a l l
    N e a t
h a r D w o r k e r
    Y e l l o w
```

NAME CRITTERS

For additional name fun, ask students to write their names in large letters on a sheet of art paper. Then have them use the letters to create their own name critter. This exercise will give students practice in writing and spelling their name, as well as reinforce fine-motor skills and creativity. You might display the works of art and encourage students to find the name in each picture.

 LISTENING FOR LETTERS

Use this call-and-response activity to encourage listening skills and letter recognition as students focus on their names.

If your name starts with **A** or **B**,
Touch your nose to your knee.

If your name starts with **C** or **D**,
Stomp your foot to the count of three.

If it starts with **E**, **F**, or **G**,
Squat, jump up, and say "That's me!"

If your name starts with **H** or **I**,
Reach up high to touch the sky.

If it starts with **J**, **K**, or **L**,
Make the sound of a ringing bell.

If your name starts with **M** or **N**,
Put your hands around your chin.

If it starts with **O**, **P**, or **Q**,
Touch your elbow to your shoe.

If your name starts with **R** or **S**,
Take a bow, or curtsy—do your best!

If it starts with **T**, **U**, or **V**,
Buzz around like a bumblebee.

And if it starts with **W**, **X**, **Y**, or **Z**,
Act as silly as you can be.

Now, to end this alphabet game,
On the count of three, call out your name!
1...2...3!

NAME GAME

In this round-robin-like name game, attentive listening skills and memory are key. In advance, prepare a name card for each child, then place the cards in a paper bag. To play, have students sit in a circle on the floor. Invite a volunteer to draw a card from the bag and read the name. Ask that student to stand up and tell something about himself or herself, such as a favorite color or activity. Then invite that child to draw the next name from the bag and name the classmate, who then tells about himself or herself. Continue in this manner until all of the names have been drawn and every child has had a turn to share. Finally, return all the cards to the bag to play again. This time, however, when students draw names, they must try to remember what that child shared about himself or herself in the first round!

 MY NAME BRAND

Point out to students that many products are labeled with the name of their inventors. For example, a popular brand of clothing—Levi's®—is named after Levi Strauss, who co-invented blue jeans in 1873. Other products named for their inventors are Steinway pianos and Ford automobiles. Invite students to "invent" a product that would carry their name. First, have them draw a picture of what their invention would look like or how it would be used. Then ask them to write about their product and tell why they invented it.

 NAME TALK

Hold a discussion about names to give students an opportunity to share what they know, think, and feel about their own names. Here are some prompts to help jumpstart the discussion:

I'm named after my grampa!

- Do you like your name? Why or why not?

- Do you like the way your name looks in print? Why or why not?

- How do you feel when you hear your name pronounced?

- Is your name easy to read and pronounce?

- Do you know what your name means? Share what you know.

- Were you named after someone special? If yes, who?

- Do you have a nickname? How did you get it?

- If you could choose your own name, would you keep the one you have? Why or why not?

- If you changed your name, what name would you choose? Explain.

★ TRAIN TRAITS

Create a train filled with unique traits about the students in your class. First, make one copy of the train engine (page 75) and a class supply of the train car (page 76) on a variety of light-colored paper. Distribute the train cars for students to cut out, label with their name, and then glue their photo to. (You might take and print out digital photos in advance.) Then ask students to write words or phrases on their car that describe themselves, such as "laughs a lot," "tall," "friendly," and " loves math." To prepare the engine, fill in your name, add your photo, and write traits about yourself on the cutout. Line up the train cars behind the engine to create a display labeled "Train Traits."

★ "BEST-OF" BALLOONS

The adorable clown on page 77 can be used to help students communicate their favorite things with the class. Copy a supply of the pattern and distribute to students. Then invite them to write the name of something they like best on each balloon. You might provide a list of topics for students to use, or let them fill in the balloons with items of their choice. Some topics for students to consider might include favorite books, holidays, foods, colors, people, places to visit, activities, and ways to travel. After they fill in the balloons, write their name, and color the clown, encourage students to share about the things they like best with the class.

★ MY "ME" BOOK

Invite students to complete this book to help raise their self-awareness. Simply copy a class supply of pages 78–87, distribute each page to students, and have them follow the directions to complete the page. (You might present students with one page per day.) When all of the pages are completed, staple each child's pages together along the left side. Then encourage students to share their books with classmates, family, and friends. These personalized books also make nice keepsakes!

Cover: Write your name in any style or way you desire.

Page 1: Draw a picture of yourself in the frame. Write your first and last name on the line and complete the sentence at the bottom.

Page 2: Complete the page by marking, writing, or coloring your responses. Decorate the child at the top to represent yourself.

Page 3: Check the box to show which hand you use for writing and drawing. Make a paint handprint of that hand in the box.

Page 4: Ask a friend to help you measure your height and different body parts. Write your findings.

Page 5: Fill in your birthday information, color the cake, and draw candles on it. Complete the sentence at the bottom of the page.

Page 6: At the top, check the box for your favorite meal and draw your favorite food in the box. Then complete the rest of the page to indicate your favorite things.

Page 7: Draw a picture of your family in the box. Complete the bottom of the page.

Page 8: At the top, draw a picture or your home or a place that you'd like to live. At the bottom, draw something in your home that you like a lot. Then draw your pet, or a pet you'd like to own. Write its name on the line.

Page 9: Draw and write about things that make you special.

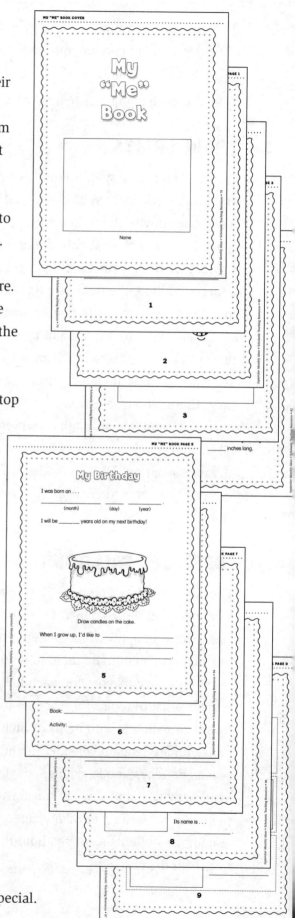

"WANTED" MINI-POSTER

Students can provide at-a-glance information about themselves with the mini-poster on page 88. To complete, have students write their first and last names at the top and draw a self-portrait in the box. Then have them fill out the personal information or dictate their responses for you to write. Once finished, invite students to share their "Wanted" bulletins with the class. If desired, display them on a bulletin board or scattered on walls, windows, and doors around the classroom.

 ## PAPER PLATE SELF-PORTRAITS

Provide 9-inch paper plates and an assortment of craft materials for students to use to create self-portraits. To begin, ask students to color the plate to match their skin tone. Then have them add other features that represent their appearance, such as wiggle eyes, yarn hair, pipe-cleaner mouth, and paper ear cutouts. When completed, give students a bow-shaped cutout to write their name on and attach to their portraits. Boys might attach the bow to the bottom of their portrait to represent a bowtie, and girls might use theirs as a hair-bow. Display the portraits on a wall or bulletin board titled, "Our Class Family."

 ## FABULOUS FAMILY MEMBERS

To help students gather information about their family, have them conduct interviews with adult family members. Copy a supply of the Family Member Interview form on page 89 and distribute several to each child. Review the items on the page, then have students take their pages home to fill out with their family members (one form per adult). After students return their interviews, encourage them to share what they learned about their family member, as well as about their family.

FAMILY COAT OF ARMS

Invite students to create a family coat of arms. Explain that a coat of arms is a shield that bears symbols, colors, and mottos that represent a particular person, family, or country. Distribute copies of page 90 for students to decorate with colors, symbols, phrases, and art that represents their family. When completed, ask volunteers to show their coat of arms and tell the class about what each element represents and why.

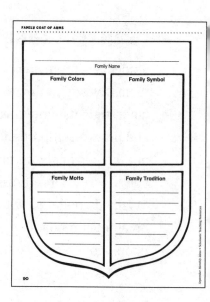

 ## FAMILY QUILT

Copy a class supply of the quilt pattern on page 91. Have students create a special family quilt by writing their family name in the center square and coloring that square with their favorite color. Have them write the name of a different family member in each of the other sections. They can include themselves, their parents, siblings, grandparents, aunts and uncles, cousins, and so on until the quilt is filled. Finally, have students color each section, then cut out the quilt. Display the quilt squares side-by-side to create a large, student-made, family quilt.

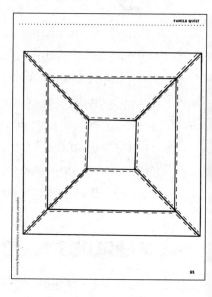

 ## GRANDPARENTS' DAY CARD

In 1978, President Jimmy Carter signed into law the resolution declaring National Grandparents' Day as the first Sunday after Labor Day. Invite students to create a card to recognize a grandparent or an older family member or friend on this special day. First, copy a supply of the card pattern (page 92) onto tagboard. Have students cut out the card, write a message to their special person on the back, and sign their name. They might also draw a picture of their special person. Next, instruct students to color the front of card, then fold the card back along the dotted lines so that the two sections of the door meet at the center. To seal, give children a 1¼- by 3-inch section of a sticky note (the part with adhesive on the back) to label "Happy Grandparents' Day" and then affix above the door on the card. Encourage students to deliver their card in person, or present it to their chosen person at a class "Tea" held in honor of their grandparents or special visitors.

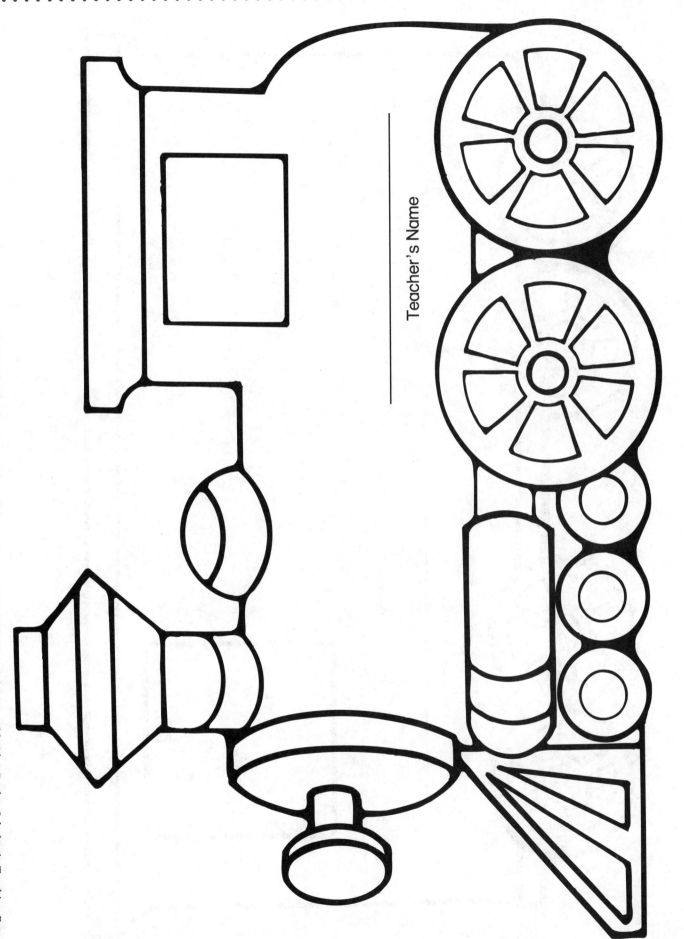

Teacher's Name

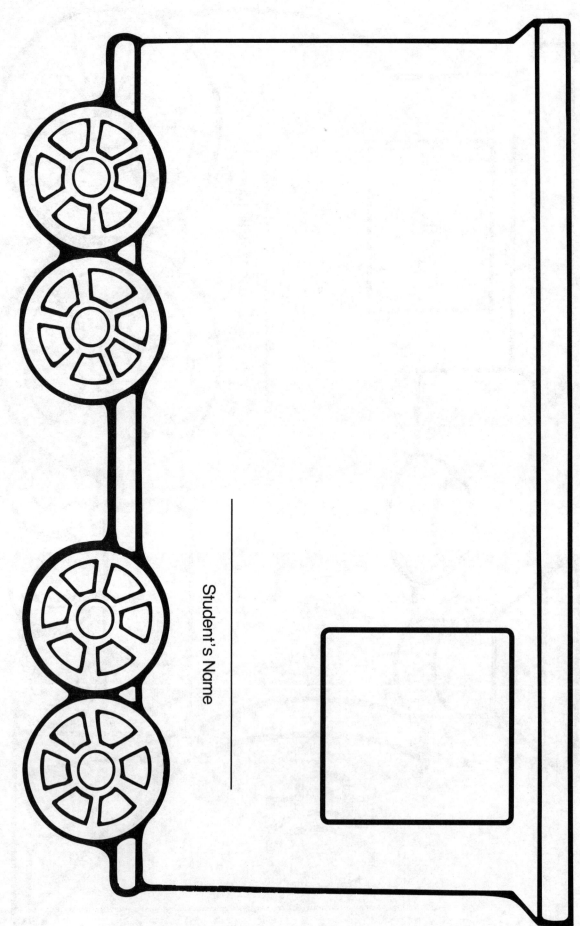

Student's Name

Student's Name

My "Me" Book

Name

My Self-Portrait

My name is . . .

_____

The best thing about me is . . .

_____

_____

_____

1

About Me

I am a . . .   ❑ girl   ❑ boy

My hair is . . .

❑ black   ❑ blonde   ❑ brown   ❑ red   ❑ other

My eyes are . . .

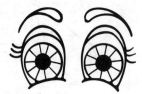

_____

(color)

I counted my teeth.

I have _____ top teeth.

I have _____ bottom teeth.

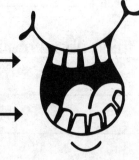

2

My Handprint

I use this hand for writing and drawing:

❏ left hand   ❏ right hand

3

My Measurements

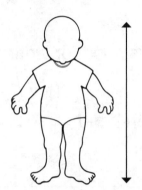

I am _____ inches tall!

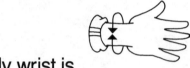

My arm is

_____ inches long.

My wrist is

_____ inches around.

My finger is

_____ inches long.

My thumb is

_____ inches long.

My leg is

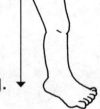

_____ inches long.

My foot is

_____ inches long.

4

My Birthday

I was born on . . .

_____ _____ _____ .
(month)   (day)   (year)

I will be _____ years old on my next birthday!

Draw candles on the cake.

When I grow up, I'd like to _____

_____

_____ .

My Favorite Things

My favorite meal is . . .

❑ breakfast   ❑ lunch   ❑ dinner

This is my favorite food.

Here are more of my favorites:

Number: _____   Color: _____

Subject: _____   Game: _____

Day of week: _____   Holiday: _____

Book: _____

Activity: _____

6

My Family

This is my family.

I have _____ brothers and _____ sisters.
       (number)   (number)

Their names are:

_____   _____

_____   _____

_____   _____

At Home

This is my home, or where I would like to live.

This item is in my home:

This is my pet:

Its name is . . .

_____ .

8

More About Me

These things make me special!

_____

_____

_____

_____

_____

_____

_____

_____

_____

9

WANTED

_____

Student's Name

Height: _____

Age: _____

Hair color: _____

Eye color: _____

School last seen at: _____

Known to hang out at: _____

_____

Known to hang out with: _____

_____

Favorite things to do: _____

_____

Family Member Interview

Family Member: _____

Relationship to me: _____

Birthdate: _____

Birthplace: _____

Occupation: _____

Favorite color: _____

Favorite holiday: _____

Favorite book: _____

_____

Favorite movie: _____

Brothers and sisters: _____

What person was like as a child: _____

_____

What person liked best about school: _____

_____

Favorite family-related memory: _____

_____

Family Name

Family Colors

Family Symbol

Family Motto

_____

_____

_____

_____

_____

Family Tradition

_____

_____

_____

_____

_____

September Monthly Idea Book © Scholastic Teaching Resources

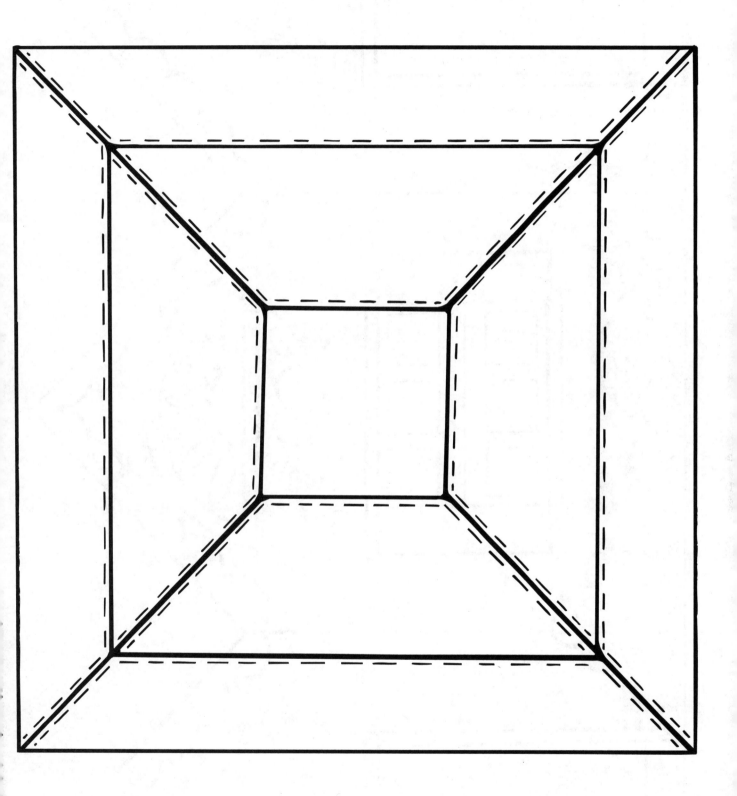

LET'S CELEBRATE BIRTHDAYS!

Birthdays are personal and special occasions for kids of all ages. In celebrating students' important day, you can help boost their sense of self while teaching essential math skills and calendar concepts. In this section, you'll find ideas that spotlight individuals on their special day, suggestions for class birthday displays and celebrations, and ways to make these important occasions a time for learning.

Suggested Activities

★ BIRTHDAY PREPARATIONS

There are many things you can do in advance so you'll be ready to shine the spotlight on children on their special day (Note: Weekend birthdays can be celebrated on Friday.). Here are a few ideas:

Royal Recognition

To recognize the birthday child, decorate his or her personal space in a royal way. For example, cover the child's chair to give it a throne-like appearance or create a special birthday coat of arms to display at the child's cubby or desk. In addition, you might make a birthday crown, cape, and scepter for the child's use on that special day.

A Present of Privileges

Label a set of cards with class privileges, such as "line leader," "class messenger," and "extra computer time." Write one privilege on each card. Place the cards in a gift-wrapped box with a separately wrapped, removable lid. Attach a bow to the lid. Present the "gift" to the birthday child. Then throughout the day, allow the child to choose cards from the box to take advantage of a particular privilege (one use per card).

Surprise Birthday Cards

Prepare birthday cards to send to students on their special day! In advance, label a separate file folder for each month of the year. Place a pre-addressed birthday card for each child in the folder for his or her birthday month. Pencil in the mailing date for the card in the top right corner of the envelope. On the last week of each month, review the file for the upcoming month to prepare the cards that need to be mailed. Add a personal note to those cards, affix stamps, and mail on the appropriate days.

Party Pack

Make each birthday child feel extra-special with a personalized pack of birthday goodies. Cover a large shoebox with birthday giftwrap. Cover the lid separately so that the box can be easily opened and used again and again. Add a ribbon to the lid. Then fill the box with birthday favors, such as a hat, horn, stickers, miniature puzzle, and yo-yo. Also include an inexpensive gift, personalized birthday card, and a treat such as a pack of crackers or pretzels. Present the party pack to students on their birthday as the class sings "Happy Birthday to You!" After the child empties the box, put it away to use for the next birthday occasion.

Birthday Bear

Dress up a cute, stuffed bear with curling ribbon, a gift tag labeled "Happy Birthday," and a birthday hat. Present the bear to the birthday child to have as a special companion for the day.

Gifts to Go

To students, their birthday is one of the most important days of the year! To prepare for that all-important day for each of your students, wrap gifts in advance so they'll be ready to go when you need them. You can purchase inexpensive items, such as pencils, erasers, balloons, whistles, and stickers to use as gifts. Insert each individual gift into a paper tube, wrap the tube in colored paper, and add ribbon. Place the gifts in a large, decorated basket. On their birthday, invite students to choose a gift from the basket as the class sings "Happy Birthday to You!"

Summer Birthday Celebrations

Plan in-school celebrations for students whose birthdays occur during the summer months. First determine which students have summer birthdays. Then decide on a different day near the end of the year to celebrate each child's special day. Check that the days do not overlap other birthdays or special end-of-year events. When each selected day arrives, surprise the summer-birthday child with the same attention and fanfare that you would bestow on any other birthday child on his or her special day.

Birthday Wrap-Up

As a grand finale to wrap up the whole year's worth of birthdays, bring in plain cupcakes, cans of frosting, and several varieties of cake sprinkles. Give each child a cupcake to frost and decorate. Then have students sing a round of "Happy Birthday to You!" to each other before they eat their birthday treat.

BIRTHDAY DISPLAYS

Set up a yearlong display to showcase students' birthdays. Then use the display to reinforce calendar concepts and math skills. Following are some suggestions for birthday displays you might use in your classroom:

The Birthday Train

Have your entire class jump aboard the "Birthday Train" with this special display. To make a train, cut out an engine shape from construction paper, then use twelve half-sheets of construction paper for the train cars. Cut out black paper wheels to attach to the engine and cars. (Or mask the print on the train patterns on pages 75–76 and make copies to use for the train.) Then label the engine with "Birthday Train" and each car with a different month of the year. Put each child's picture and name on the train car labeled with the month for his or her birthday. To display, sequence the cars behind the engine. Use the train as a reminder of students' birthdays throughout the year, as well as to reinforce the names, sequence, and spelling of the months of the year.

Cake-and-Candle Celebrations

Use the cake and candle patterns (page 98) for a yummy-looking birthday-cake display featuring students' birthdays. To begin, enlarge and color the birthday cake. Also, make enlarged copies of the candle (one per child) on colored paper. Label each candle with a child's name and birth date. Display the cake in a prominent place and top it with the candles for the current month. Change the candles each month. As you point out the birthdays for the month, encourage students to find those dates on the calendar and tell on which day of the week each birthday falls.

95

Birthdays by the Month

Setting up a display for monthly birthdays is as easy as 1, 2, 3 with this idea! First, fold 12 sheets of construction paper in half and glue to create pockets. Label each pocket with a different month. Cut a 9-inch length of sentence strip for each child and write the child's name and birth date on it. Slip each strip into the pocket corresponding to the child's birthday month. To display, sequence the pockets and add a "Happy Birthday" banner and large construction-paper birthday cake. (Or enlarge and color the cake pattern on page 98.) Each month, remove the sentence strips from that month's pocket and display them, ordering the strips by the birthdays that occur during the month. Use the display for math practice, such as finding the number of days between students' birthdays in that month and counting the days until the next birthday arrives.

Birthday Cupcake

Make 12 enlarged copies of the cupcake patterns (page 99) on different colors of paper. Label each cupcake top with a different month. On the cupcake bottom, write the name of each student who has a birthday in that month and the date of his or her birthday. Assemble and sequence the cupcakes to create a display. If desired, top each cupcake with a construction-paper candle.

 ## FOR THE BIRTHDAY CHILD

The following activities give children an opportunity to create something special for their own or a classmate's birthday.

Birthday Visor

Copy the visor pattern (page 100) onto tagboard or a light color of construction paper. Invite the birthday child to cut out and color the visor, adding candles to match his or her age. To assemble, punch a hole in both ends of the visor where indicated, and attach a length of elasticized string or yarn. Fit the visor to the child's head as you tie the string into place.

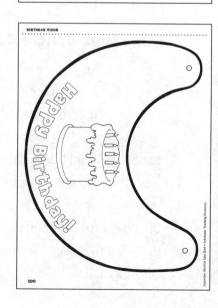

Giant Birthday Card

Make a class card to present to the birthday child. In advance, enlarge and cut out the birthday card pattern on page 101. Then fold a large sheet of white construction paper in half. Glue the card along the fold where indicated, centering it vertically along the fold. Without the birthday child's knowledge, have small groups take turns adding their own decorations and birthday greetings to the card. They might add a circus scene on the front of the card around the clown, or draw balloons or other clowns to fill in the space. Once the card is completed, set it aside, out of the birthday child's sight. When the special day arrives, have the class present the card with a lively round of "Happy Birthday to You!"

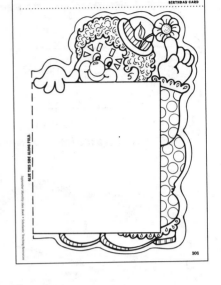

Wishing Mobile

Have the birthday child, or the entire class, make these mobiles filled with birthday wishes. To begin, copy the mobile patterns (pages 102–103) onto sturdy paper for students to color and cut out. Ask them to label the cake with their name. On the back of each gift, have them write about a wish they would make on their birthday. When finished, instruct students to attach the gifts to the cake with tape and yarn. (Each piece of yarn should be a different length.) Have them create a yarn loop to attach to the top of the cake. You can have only the birthday child create a mobile on his or her birthday, or have small groups each take a gift and write wishes for the birthday child on the back. Or, you might ask all students to make their own mobile on the same day, then feature a child's mobile on his or her birthday.

Celebrate With a Certificate

Copy and fill out the certificate (page 104) to present to children on their birthday. On the lines at the bottom, write a special birthday greeting, wish, or words of praise about the birthday child. If desired, copy a class supply and invite each child to create a personalized certificate to give to the birthday child.

Name

Birth Date

Happy Birthday!

MARCH
Ann 5th
Tim 14th

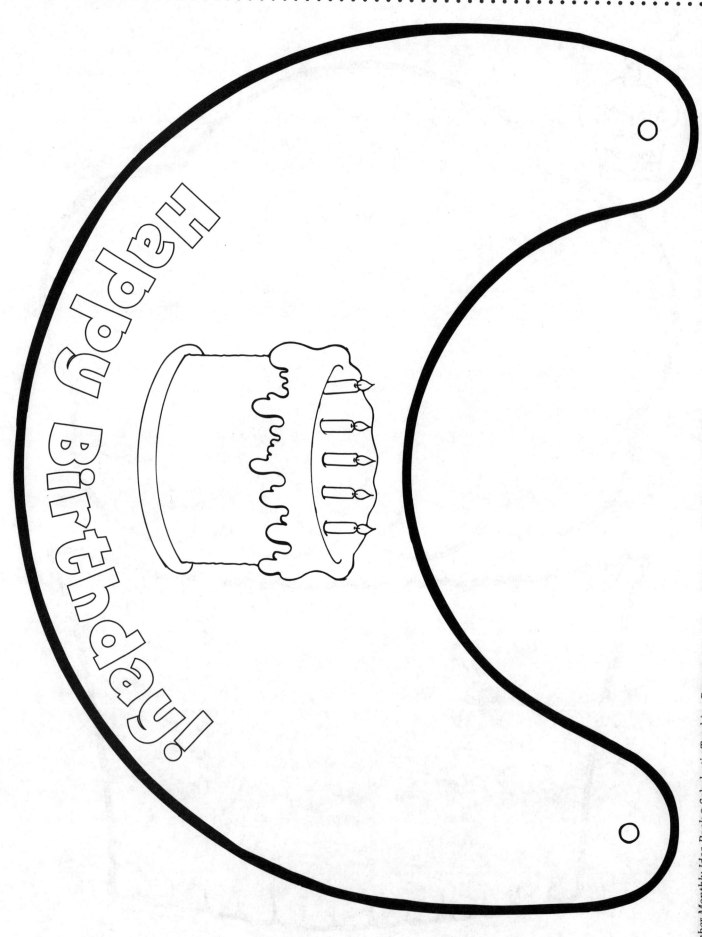

Happy Birthday!

GLUE THIS SIDE ALONG FOLD.

Congratulations!

It's

_____
Student's Name

BIRTHDAY!

September Monthly Idea Book • Scholastic Teaching Res…

APPLE TIME

John Chapman, better known as Johnny Appleseed, was born in Massachusetts on September 26, 1774. Appleseed earned his nickname from selling and planting apple trees throughout the Midwest. In his travels, this American pioneer made friends with settlers and Native Americans in the region. Many towns were established near the apple orchards he helped plant. Appleseed's widespread reputation made him a legendary figure whose activities prompted a number of tall tales about him.

Because of Appleseed's contribution to introducing apple trees to settlements in Ohio, Indiana, and Illinois, it seems fitting that he was born during the apple-harvest season. Apples are a favorite fall topic of study in early education classrooms, and the theme is used to teach and reinforce skills in science, math, language arts, and social studies.

Suggested Activities

 ### JOHNNY APPLESEED FACTS

Appleseed was born on September 26, 1774.

Share the information about Johnny Appleseed (above) with students. Write each fact about him on an apple cutout. (You might enlarge the apples on page 110 for this purpose.) Then invite your class to conduct research—using the Internet and other sources—to learn more about Johnny Appleseed. Invite them to label additional apple cutouts with their findings (one fact per apple). Finally, use the fact apples to create a display about this historical figure.

 ### APPLESAUCE TREAT

In honor of Johnny Appleseed, and to practice measurement skills, invite students to help make this simple applesauce recipe.

APPLESAUCE TREAT

I qt. apples, peeled and sliced

I cup water

½ cup sugar

I tsp. lemon juice

¼ tsp. cinnamon

pinch of salt

Combine all ingredients in a saucepan. Cook until apples are tender. Allow to cool, then mash with a potato masher or electric mixer. Serve cold.

(makes 8–10 servings)

APPLE DISCOVERIES

Bring in a variety of apples, such as Fuji, Gala, Granny Smith, Golden Delicious, Macintosh, Red Delicious, and Winesap. Cut each apple type in half and show students the seeds inside. Discuss the different parts of the apple. (Cut a few apples crosswise to reveal the star pattern of the seeds.) Then peel and cut the apples into bite-sized pieces. Place each kind on a paper plate labeled with its name. Set out the plates, and invite students to taste each apple. Do they all taste the same? Afterward, take a vote to find out which apple is the class favorite. Make a class graph to show the results.

 ## APPLE MOBILE

For these hanging decorations, copy the mobile patterns (page 108) onto the following colors of paper: the leaf on green, the apple top and bottom on white, and the core on yellow. Have students cut out the patterns, color the apple top and bottom in the color of their choice, and write words on the patterns that describe apples. If they participated in "Apple Discoveries" (above), they might label the leaf with their favorite type of apple and write descriptions for that apple on the other patterns. To add textural interest, they might glue real apple seeds to the core. To assemble, have students glue each of their patterns to a length of yarn, as shown.

 ## LIFT-THE-FLAP APPLE MYSTERIES

Make tagboard templates of the apple patterns on page 109. Have students fold red construction paper in half, trace the template onto the paper— aligning the straight edge along the fold—and cut out the shape through both layers of paper. Have them trace the leaf onto green paper and cut it out. Then ask students to choose a mystery object or person. Have them write clues about their choice on the outside of the apple and draw or glue a picture of it under the flap. Next, have students write their name on the stem and glue it to the folded edge of their apple. Invite them to challenge classmates to guess their mystery item or person, and then lift the flap to check the answer.

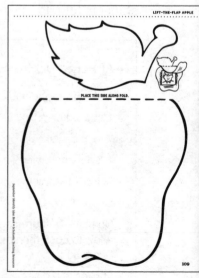

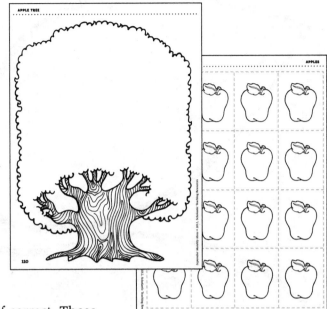

APPLE TREE SKILLS

Teach and reinforce a variety of skills with the apple tree and apple patterns (pages 110–111). You can label a supply of apples with math facts and write the answers on the back. Or write sight words on the apples. To use, color and copy the tree pattern, laminate, and use it as a work mat. Then program the cards (laminate for repeated use) and have students place them on the tree. They can "pick" an apple, respond to the particular task, and keep the apple if correct. These customized activities are perfect for learning centers or independent practice!

 WRITE ABOUT IT!

Encourage students to write about Johnny Appleseed, apples, apple orchards, or just write an apple-related story. Have them use the apple stationery (page 112) for their final copy. To make the writing sheet readily available, copy and place a supply of the stationery in a basket topped with an apple-themed ribbon or bow. If desired, prepare a bulletin board with an apple border to display student work.

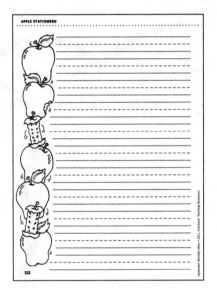

APPLE OF MY EYE

Students can use the apple pattern (page 113) to write notes of praise, congratulations, and encouragement to others (including the teacher!). Copy and keep a supply of the pattern on hand for use at any time. To use, students simply cut out the apple, fill out the front, write their message on the back, and present the apple to share their words of praise or encouragement.

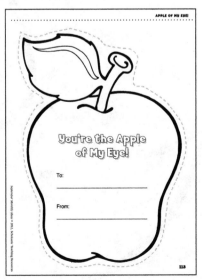

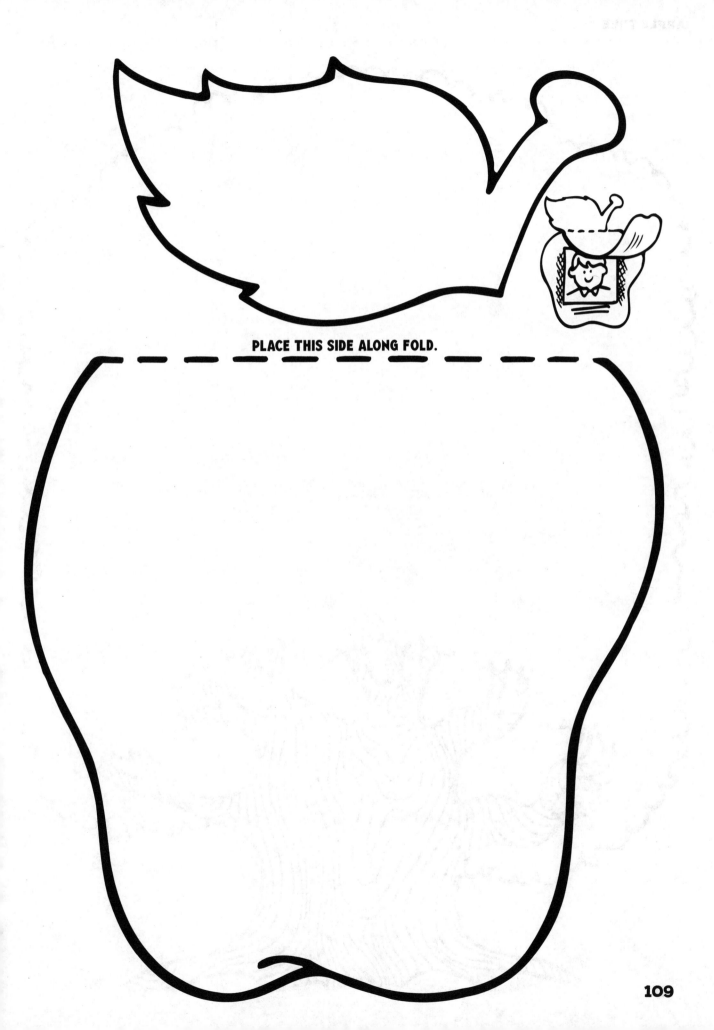

PLACE THIS SIDE ALONG FOLD.

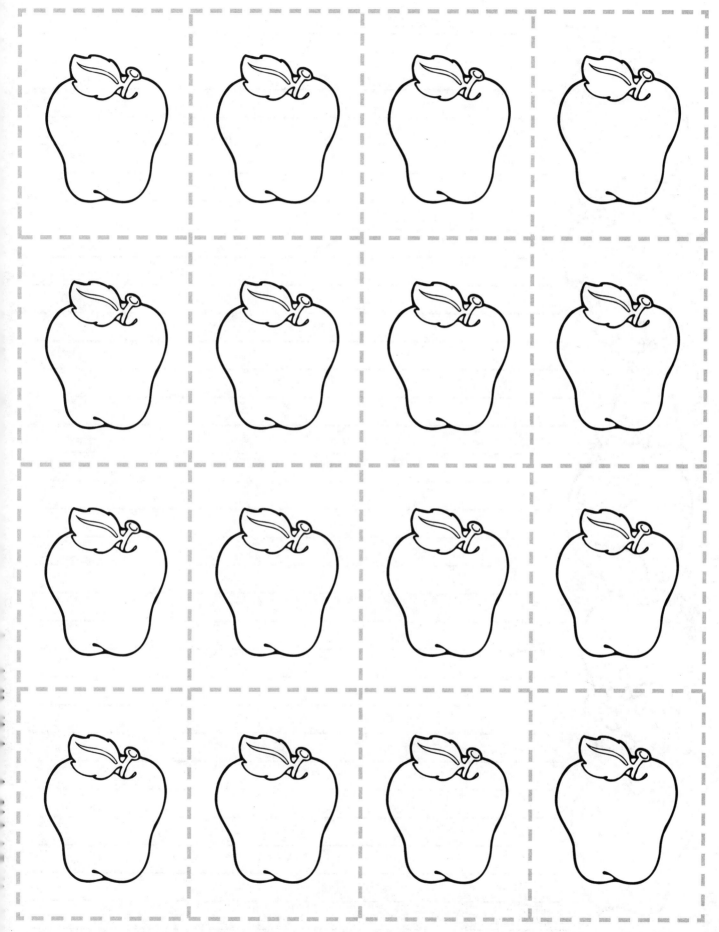

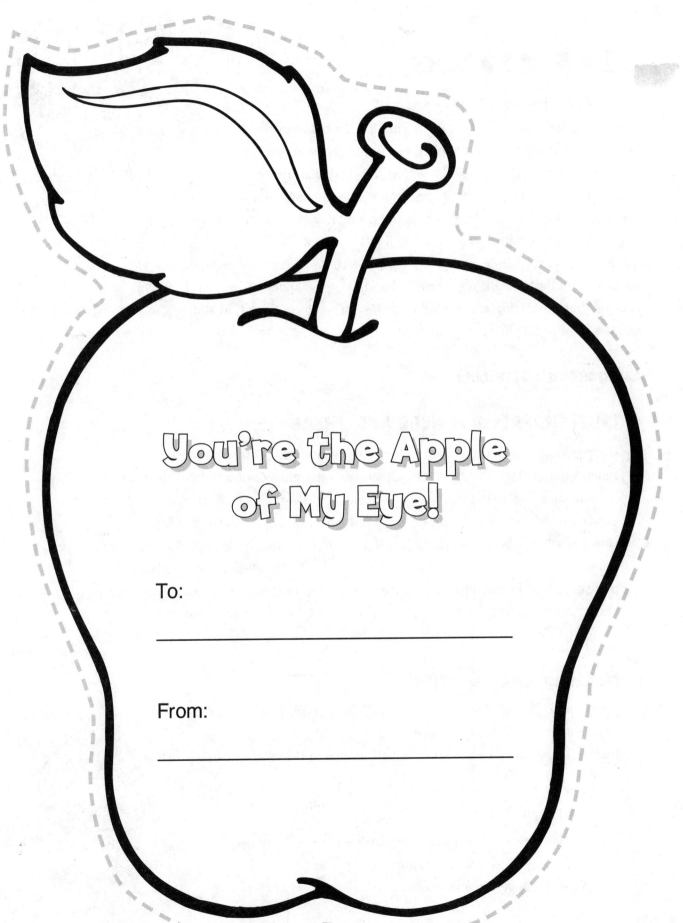

You're the Apple of My Eye!

To:

_____

From:

_____

VIVA MEXICO!

In Mexico, September 16—*Diez y Seis de Septiembre*—marks Independence Day. On this day in 1810, Father Miguel Hidalgo y Costilla rang a church bell to call Mexicans to fight for their freedom from the Spaniards, who ruled Mexico at the time. Every year, this holiday is commemorated with a re-enactment of the ringing of the bell in plazas across the country. The square in Mexico City is decorated with flags and lights in the official colors of the country: red, white, and green. People gather in communities around Mexico to participate in fiestas featuring mariachi bands, dancers, parades, rodeos, bullfights, and charros (horseback riders). And there's plenty of traditional food, in addition to the goodies used to fill piñatas for the kids!

Suggested Activities

 ## INDEPENDENCE DAY HERE AND THERE

Have students conduct research to learn more about the history of Mexico's Independence Day. As they work, ask students to think about ways the Mexican holiday compares to our country's Independence Day holiday. What events led to each country's revolt and fight for freedom? How did the day become a holiday? How is each holiday recognized and celebrated? If desired, divide the class into two groups and assign each group one of the countries to research. Have the groups prepare murals to illustrate and describe their country's Independence Day history and celebrations. Display the murals side by side so students can describe and compare information about the two countries.

 ## MEXICAN COAT OF ARMS

Distribute copies of Mexico's coat of arms (page 117). Explain that the images on this country symbol have special meanings. Share the meanings (below), then invite students to color their copy of the coat of arms.

- *Golden Eagle:* This national bird represents the Mexican people—their strength and nobility.

- *Snake:* This creature depicts Mexico's enemies. The eagle is devouring the snake, indicating the Mexican people will be victorious over their enemies.

- *Cactus:* This thorny cactus symbolizes Mexico's trials and challenges. The eagle stands on it to represent the people's will to overcome their troubles.

- *Pedestal:* The figure under the cactus symbolizes Mexico's origins—the different cultures that came together and formed the foundation of the country.

- *Laurel and oak leaves:* These represent the victories of the people and those who gave their lives for the country.

★ MAP OF MEXICO

Help students find Mexico on a globe or large world map. Identify other countries and bodies of water that connect to or surround the country. Also, talk about on which continent the country lies. Then point out and name important Mexican landforms that are visible on the map. To sum up your geography lesson, distribute the map of Mexico (page 118) for students to complete. Encourage them to refer to the globe or map, as needed.

★ MEXICO FACT FINDER

Have students complete the activities on page 119 to learn more about Mexico and its culture, history, and language. Encourage them to use resources, such as the Internet, encyclopedias, and nonfiction books. When finished, ask students to share and compare their answers.

★ SPANISH WORD FIND

Distribute a copy of the Spanish Word Find (page 120) to students and explain that the word bank contains Spanish words associated with Mexican culture. Have them find and circle those words in their word-find puzzle. After they complete the activity, ask students to define each word. Provide Spanish-English dictionaries and other resources for students to use for research. They can write each word and its definition on the back of their page.

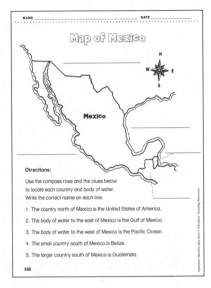

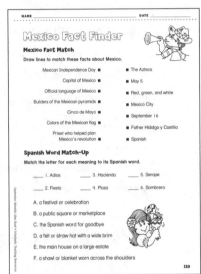

MAGNIFICENT MEXICO!

Students can complete page 121 to show off their knowledge of Mexico. Have them use what they've already learned about the country in addition to information gathered from resources, such as books, the Internet, and encyclopedias. When finished, invite students to share their pages with the class. If desired, have them draw pictures to go with their information pages, then display their work on a bulletin board titled, "Viva Mexico!"

 ## MEXICO BOOKLET

Liven up writing assignments about Mexico by providing students with the themed book cover (page 122) and stationery (page 123). Encourage them to write about Mexico's people, culture, customs, holidays, geography, agriculture, or any other country-related topic. Invite volunteers to share their writing with classmates.

 ## PAPER-BAG PINATA

Making this bull piñata is quick and easy. Simply nest two or three large paper bags inside each other and fill with treats, such as small party favors, scratch and sniff stickers, erasers, pencils, free-homework passes, and individually wrapped snacks. Fold the top of the bag over a sturdy wire coat hanger and staple in place. Then copy the bull patterns (page 124) onto construction paper, cut them out, and glue to the bag as shown. Also, make a pair of construction-paper ears for the bull. Use heavy cord or rope to suspend the piñata from a tree limb or clothesline. Invite students to take turns striking the piñata until it breaks open.

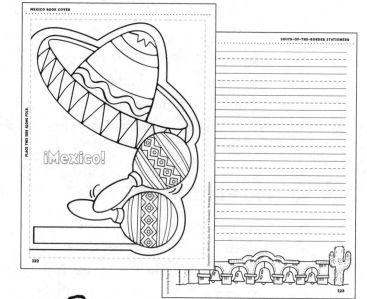

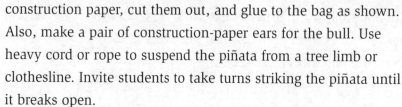

Map of Mexico

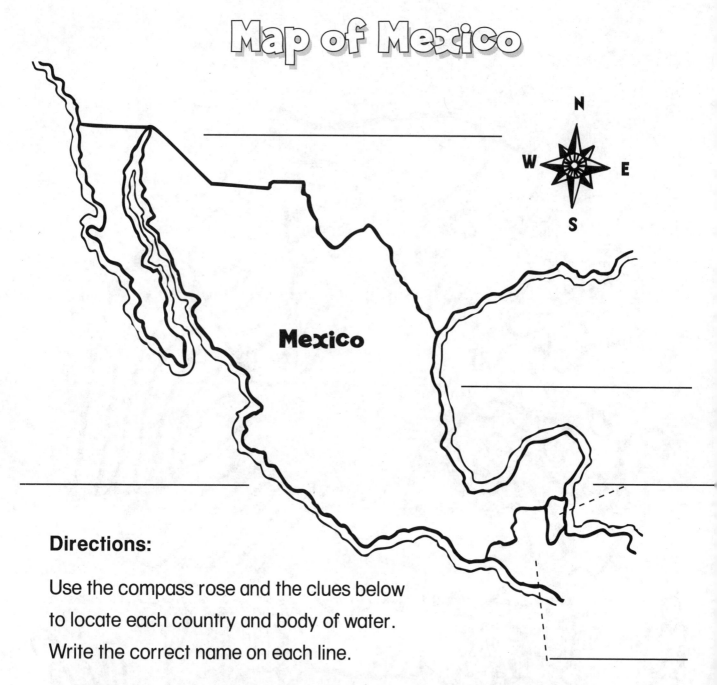

Mexico

N
W E
S

Directions:

Use the compass rose and the clues below
to locate each country and body of water.
Write the correct name on each line.

1. The country north of Mexico is the United States of America.

2. The body of water to the east of Mexico is the Gulf of Mexico.

3. The body of water to the west of Mexico is the Pacific Ocean.

4. The small country south of Mexico is Belize.

5. The larger country south of Mexico is Guatemala.

Mexico Fact Finder

Mexico Fact Match

Draw lines to match these facts about Mexico.

Mexican Independence Day ■   ■ The Aztecs

Capital of Mexico ■   ■ May 5

Official language of Mexico ■   ■ Red, green, and white

Builders of the Mexican pyramids ■   ■ Mexico City

Cinco de Mayo ■   ■ September 16

Colors of the Mexican flag ■   ■ Father Hidalgo y Costilla

Priest who helped plan
Mexico's revolution ■   ■ Spanish

Spanish Word Match-Up

Match the letter for each meaning to its Spanish word.

_____ 1. Adios   _____ 3. Hacienda   _____ 5. Serape

_____ 2. Fiesta   _____ 4. Plaza   _____ 6. Sombrero

A. a festival or celebration

B. a public square or marketplace

C. the Spanish word for goodbye

D. a felt or straw hat with a wide brim

E. the main house on a large estate

F. a shawl or blanket worn across the shoulders

Spanish Word Find

Find these words in the puzzle below:

ADIOS   BRONCO   CASA   ESPAÑOL
FIESTA   HACIENDA   MESA   PIÑATA
PLAZA   SEÑOR   SERAPE   SEÑORITA
SOMBRERO   TORTILLA

```
R T E F I E S T A A C V B N M J K H G F D S A E
C S T Y U I D F G H J K L M N B M P L A Z A P L
A W R T Y B G H D S R T H J K L O I U N B G T Y
S W C V A D I O S E T H Y U I K A S D F G H J T
A F V B N M C X Z R F S A W E P I Ñ A T A M B V
A W E R T G H Y U A T G B F D S A E R T F D S A
W C X Z D F R T H P J U P L I W R T G H M R T Y
R T Y U D E R T H E K I B R O N C O E R E W T U
E S P A Ñ O L E F G H L K D F M N B G F S W Y Y
K M S W C V B N M J K L P O I U Y T R E A E F R
W V F T H Y J U S Y U K I L O K T O R T I L L A
A S D F R T H Y O D R T H Y U J K I O L P L M K
W S A E C R F G M S A E T H A C I E N D A T H Y
E R Y H N G R F B K M Z X C V B N M L K J H G F
W E R T H Y J U R K S E T H Y J U I K L O Y H T
S E Ñ O R S W E E A W E R T Y U I O P L K J H G
Q W E R T D C V R T G B N H Y U J M W R T Y H U
W S D E R T B V O A S E R C V S E Ñ O R I T A Y
```

NAME ______________________________ DATE ______________

Magnificent Mexico!

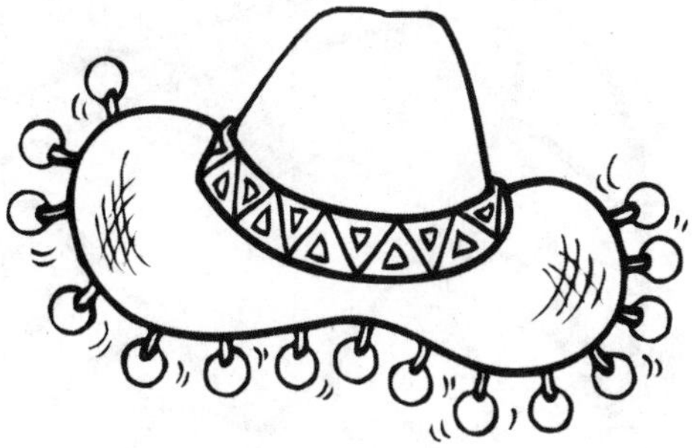

Capital city: ______________________________

National language: ______________________________

Neighboring countries: ______________________________

____

____

Tell about a Mexican holiday: ______________________________

____

____

____

Tell about a famous Mexican: ______________________________

____

____

____

Describe a Mexican tradition or food: ______________________________

____

____

____

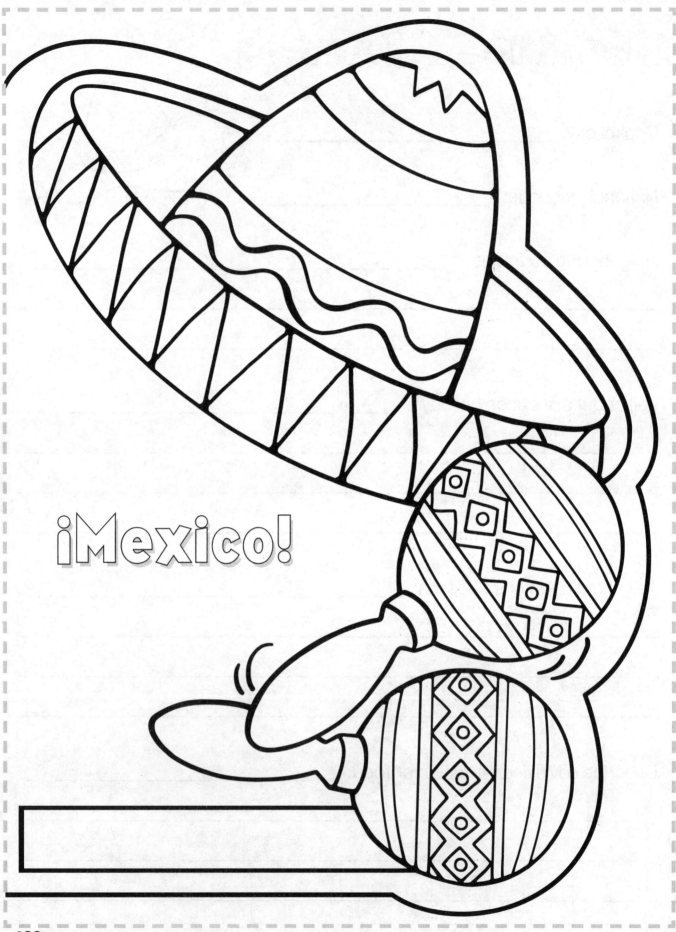

¡Mexico!

NATIVE NORTH AMERICANS

Over the years, designated days to celebrate and commemorate the contributions, culture, and history of the American Indian have occurred in September, although around the country, states held observances in different months. However, in 2009, Congress passed legislation establishing the Friday after Thanksgiving as Native American Heritage Day.

Suggested Activities

 ## NATIVE AMERICAN CULTURAL REGIONS

Christopher Columbus first gave the name "Indians" to Native Americans when he discovered what is now known as North America. At the time, Columbus had mistakenly believed that he had reached the Indies. The United States is divided into seven cultural regions in which tribes share similar surroundings and natural resources, and have very similar kinds of culture. Below is a brief description of each region and the lives of Native Americans who inhabited the area before Europeans arrived.

The Northwest Coast Region

This area covers the coast of California, Oregon, Washington, and parts of Canada. The Native Americans here lived in plank houses in large villages. Four or five families lived in one house. The tribes fished for salmon and hunted large sea animals, such as seals and whales, in the Pacific Ocean. They also hunted deer, bear, and mountain sheep and goats.

The Plateau Region

Idaho and parts of Oregon and Washington were home to Native Americans in this region, which is located between the Cascade and Rocky Mountains. Natives moved from place to place throughout the year. They lived in sunken lodges in winter and above-ground longhouses in the summer. They fished the many rivers for salmon and gathered edible fruits and vegetables.

The California-Intermountain Region

This region extends from the Pacific Coast to the Sierra Nevada Mountains and into the Great Basin. Tribes in the northern part of the region lived in sunken longhouses in winter and mat houses made of grass and branches in summer. They fished and hunted sheep and deer. Natives in the rest of the region moved around, building their homes from branches, grass, and twigs. They gathered food and hunted small animals. Tribes in this region were excellent basket weavers.

The Southwest Region

The Native Americans of this area lived in the present-day states of Arizona, New Mexico, and Colorado. Most tribes farmed and grew crops, such as corn and beans. They also hunted rabbits, wild turkey, and other small animals. Many lived in villages where their apartment-like homes were made of stone and adobe (sun-dried clay). Natives here wove baskets and blankets, made pottery, and created colorful sand paintings.

The Plains Region

This is by far the largest Native American area. It extends from the Mississippi River Valley to the Rocky Mountains and from Canada to Mexico. Natives here lived in small tribes that followed the bison herds. They also gathered wild plants for food. Tribes in this region were great horsemen and were noted for their feathered headdresses and portable tepee houses.

The Eastern Woodlands Region

This area covered the state of Minnesota and parts of southern Canada. It extended south to North Carolina and east to the Atlantic Ocean. The heavily forested areas of this region provided the Native Americans with abundant game for hunting and wood for building homes and canoes. Tribes caught fish from the many lakes and rivers, and they grew crops, such as corn, squash, and beans.

The Southeast Region

The Native Americans of this area lived in parts of Texas, along the Gulf of Mexico, and throughout the South eastward to the coastline of the Atlantic Ocean. They lived mainly in thatched-roof houses in permanent settlements. Many tribes in this region grew crops such as corn, squash, and beans for food. They also hunted, fished, and gathered wild plants. Natives in this region made beautiful handicrafts.

NATIVE AMERICANS WORD FIND

Distribute copies of the Native Americans Word Find (page 129) to each student. Point out that the word bank contains the names of Native American tribes. Instruct students to search the puzzle to find and then circle all of the names. Have them write a response to the statement below the word find puzzle. They can continue their writing on the back, if more space is needed.

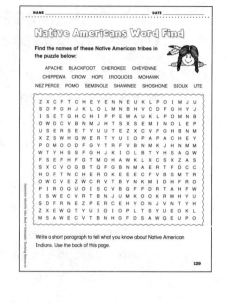

 CULTURAL REGIONS MAP

After completing the word find, give students a copy of the map on page 130. Explain that the map is roughly divided into the seven cultural regions of the United States. Working individually or in groups, students will do research to discover in which cultural regions each of the Native American tribes (listed on the word find) lived. Have them write the tribe names in the appropriate areas on the map. Encourage students to also include names of other tribes that lived in each region.

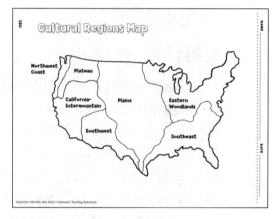

NATIVE AMERICAN REPORTS

With this research assignment, students will select and learn about a Native American people of their choice. As they research their tribe, encourage students to use classroom materials, the library, Internet, and other resources, such as videos and personal interviews. Distribute a copy of the Native American Report (page 131) to each student. As a group, discuss ways in which students can find out key information and fill in the report. When students are finished researching and writing about their tribe, invite volunteers to share their findings. Collect the reports and bind them into a class book that students can read again and again.

TRADITIONAL-DRESS NATIVE AMERICAN PUPPETS

To complement their Native American reports, provide students with copies of the puppet patterns on pages 132–133 to cut out and decorate. Students can also use the patterns as models to create their own Native American puppets, changing features and dress to suit their tribe. Provide students with large craft sticks (for handles) and an assortment of craft materials (for example, scraps of cloth, wrapping paper, or lace) for decorating their puppets. As an alternative, students might use the patterns to make posters that represent their tribe.

WRITING SYMBOLS

There were hundreds of different languages spoken by the various Native American tribes. Some languages were fairly simple, while others were quite complex. None of the native languages had a writing system until the European settlers arrived. However, many used picture symbols as part of their communication system. Ask students to review the writing symbols on page 134. Explain that these represent picture symbols that some tribes may have used. Then challenge students to use the symbols, or create some of their own, in their writings about Native Americans.

NATIVE AMERICAN STATIONERY

Liven up students' writing assignments with stationery ideal for writing about Native Americans. Copy a supply of the stationery on page 135 and place in a folder labeled "Native American Stationery." Keep the folder in a handy place so students can get the pages they will need for their writing.

Native Americans Word Find

Find the names of these Native American tribes in the puzzle below:

APACHE   BLACKFOOT   CHEROKEE   CHEYENNE

CHIPPEWA   CROW   HOPI   IROQUOIS   MOHAWK

NEZ PERCE   POMO   SEMINOLE   SHAWNEE   SHOSHONE   SIOUX   UTE

```
Z X C F T C H E Y E N N E U K L P O I M J U
S D F G H J K L O L M N B H V C D F G H Y J
I S E T G H C H I P P E W A U K L P O M N B
O W D C V B N M J H T S X S E M I N O L E P
U S E R S E T Y U U T E Z X C V F G H B N M
X Z S W H Q W E R T Y U I O P A P A C H E Y
P O M O O D F G Y T R F V B N M K J H N M M
W T Y H S S F G H J K I O L B T Y H S A Q W
F S E F H F G T M O H A W K L X C S X Z A S
S X C V O G B T Q F G B N M A E R T F D C C
H D F T N C H E R O K E E E C F V B S M T R
O W C V E Z W C R V T B Y N K M I D H F R O
P I R O Q U O I S C V B G F F D R T A H F W
I S W E C V R T B N J U M K O O K R W H Y U
S D F R N E Z P E R C E H Y O N J V N T Y H
Z X E W Q T Y U I O I O P L T S Y U E O K L
M S A W E C V T B N H G F D S A W Q E U P O
```

Write a short paragraph to tell what you know about Native American

Indians. Use the back of this page.

Cultural Regions Map

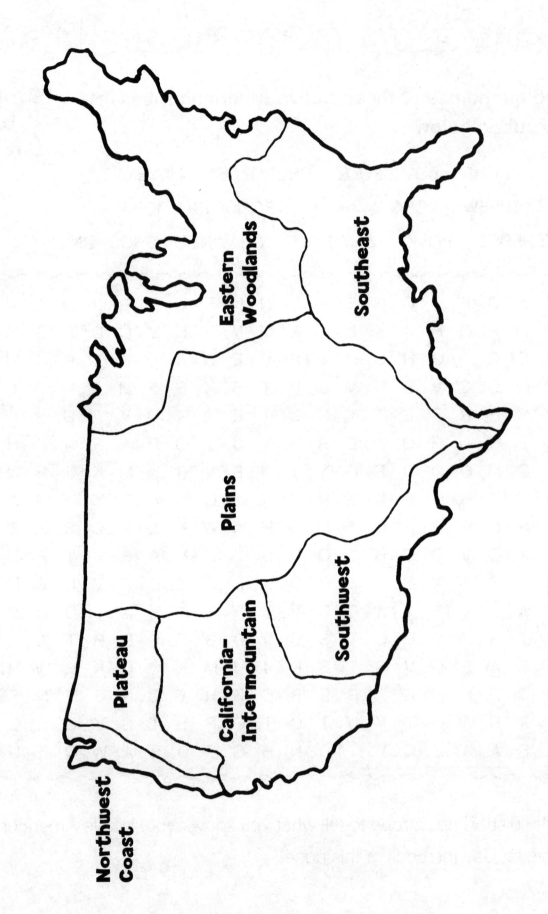

Northwest Coast

Plateau

California–Intermountain

Plains

Southwest

Eastern Woodlands

Southeast

Native American Report

_____

(Native American tribe)

1. Where did the tribe live? _____

_____

2. What kind of homes did the tribe build? _____

_____

3. What foods did the tribe eat? _____

_____

4. What crafts did the tribe make? _____

_____

5. Tell about a famous person from this tribe. _____

_____

6. What is the most interesting thing about this tribe? _____

_____

Do More!

On a separate sheet of paper, draw a person from this tribe in traditional dress. Or draw a typical home or village of the tribe.

basket	bear prints	bird
chief	clouds	deer
food	friends	hill
hunt	rain	running water
summer	tepee	war

AWARDS, INCENTIVES, AND MORE

Getting Started

Make several photocopies of the reproducibles on pages 138 through 142. Giving out the bookmarks, pencil toppers, notes, and certificates will show students your enthusiasm for their efforts and achievements. Plus, bookmarks and pencil toppers are a fun treat for students celebrating birthdays.

- Provide materials for decorating, including markers, color pencils, and stickers.

- Encourage students to bring home their creations to share and celebrate with family members.

★ BOOKMARKS

1. Photocopy onto tagboard and cut apart.

2. For more fanfare, punch a hole on one end and tie on a length of colorful ribbon or yarn.

★ PENCIL TOPPERS

1. Photocopy onto tagboard and cut out.

2. Use an art knife to cut through the Xs.

3. Slide a pencil through the Xs as shown.

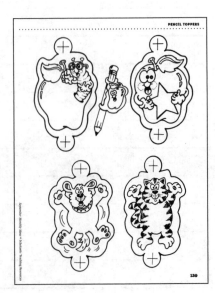

★ SEND-HOME NOTES

1. Photocopy and cut apart.

2. Record the child's name and the date.

3. Add your signature.

4. Add more details about the student's day on the back of the note.

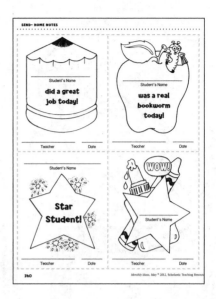

★ CERTIFICATES

1. Photocopy.

2. Record the child's name and other information, as directed.

3. Add details about the child's achievement, (if applicable), then add your signature and the date.

Whooo loves to read?

ME!

Name

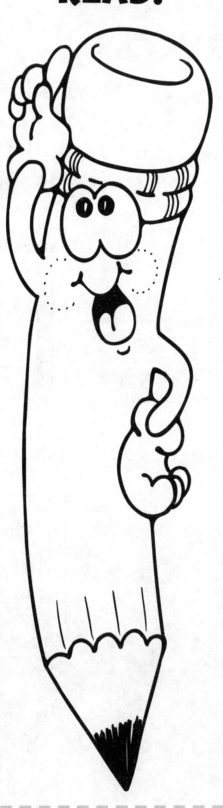

Find the facts!
READ!

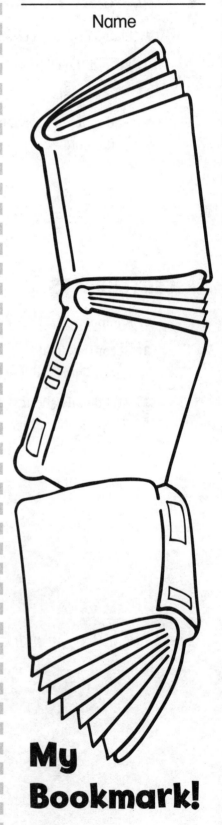

Name

My Bookmark!

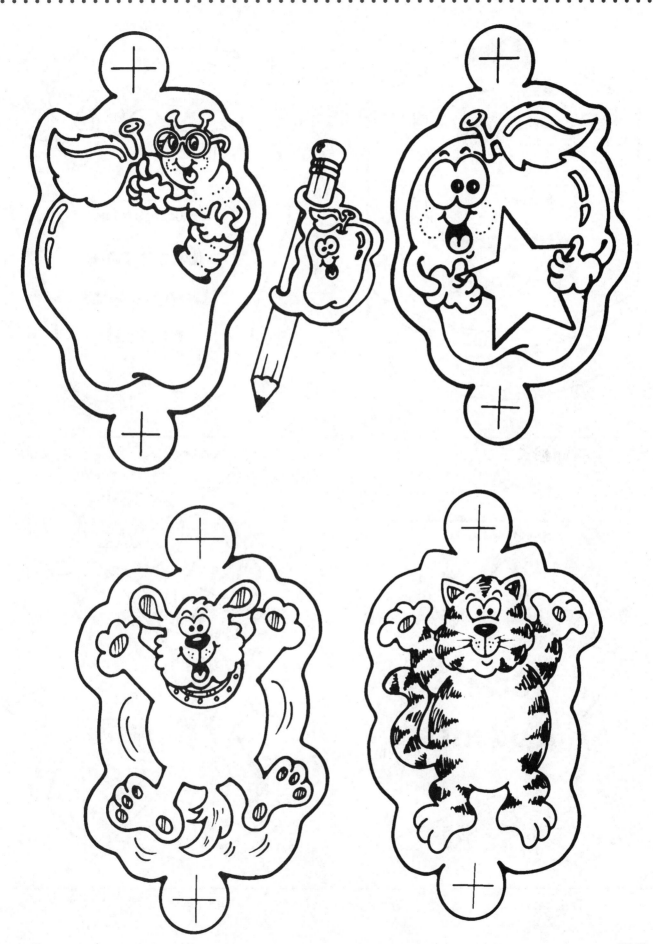

_____
Student's Name

did a great job today!

_____   _____
Teacher   Date

_____
Student's Name

was a real bookworm today!

_____   _____
Teacher   Date

_____
Student's Name

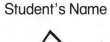

Star Student!

_____   _____
Teacher   Date

_____
Student's Name

_____   _____
Teacher   Date

Monthly Ideas, May © 2012, Scholastic Teaching Res

Student of the Week

Name _____

School _____

Teacher _____

Date _____

Certificate of Achievement

presented to

Name _____

in recognition of

_____

Teacher _____

Date _____

Back-to-School Word Find, page 67

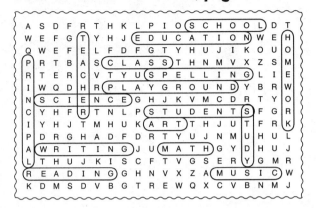

Map of Mexico, page 118

Mexico Fact Finder, page 119

1. C, 2. A, 3. E, 4. B, 5. F, 6. D

Spanish Word Find, page 120

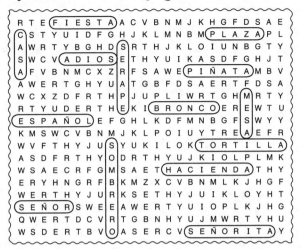

Native Americans Word Find, page 129

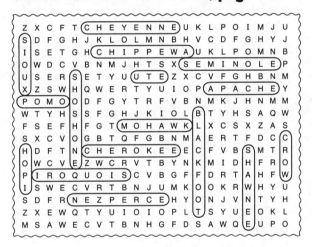

NOTES